News Journali

Nick Varley is the *Guardian*'s Sports Correspondent, reporting on sport-related news. Previously he freelanced in the newsrooms of the *Daily Mail* and the *Independent on Sunday*, among others, after working on local papers for five years. He spent three years on the *Northern Echo*, in district offices in Middlesbrough, and two years on the *Citizen* in Gloucester. His vocational training, a National Council for the Training of Journalists course in Cardiff, came after a politics and economic history degree.

Also by the author

Golden Boy: A Biography of Wilf Mannion

News
Journalism

Nick Varley

FOURTH ESTATE • *London*

First published in Great Britain in 1997 by
Fourth Estate Limited
6 Salem Road
London W2 4BU

Copyright © 1997 Fourth Estate Limited

10 9 8 7 6 5 4 3 2 1

The right of Nick Varley to be identified as the author of this work has
been asserted by him in accordance with the Copyright, Designs
and Patents Act 1988.

A catalogue record for this book is available from the British
Library.

ISBN 1-85702-693-4

Typeset by York House Typographic Ltd, London
Printed in Great Britain by Clays Ltd, St. Ives plc

Contents

Acknowledgements

Many organisations and individuals provided invaluable help in compiling this book; most of them are mentioned in the text. In addition, the author would like to thank in particular Clive Priddle, Peter Sands, Bernie Corbett, Richard Beamish, Graeme Smith, Lynne Wilson, Gary Younge, Alex Bellos and, most of all, Marianne Jones.

Introduction

Everyone knows what journalists look like and what they do, thanks, ironically, to the media. They are cynical, semi-drunk, middle-aged white men – albeit ones as aggressive as rott-weilers – recognisable by markings such as a dirty mac and a trilby with a press card in the band, all according to *Spitting Image*. Or they are a mixture of the hapless, hopeless and shameless, if you prefer the *Drop the Dead Donkey* image.

The truth is rather different – although it should be said that both the stereotypes do have several real-life incarnations. Many journalists are youngish – a third are under thirty-five, although more than half are between thirty-five and fifty-four – and, while women are under-represented, they still account for 36 per cent of the profession.

The one area where the TV images are all too true is in the absence of black faces: just 1.6 per cent of the survey of more than 6,400 members of the National Union of Journalists (NUJ), from which all the figures quoted above are taken. But the union and others in the industry are trying to address an imbalance which cannot be healthy for a business which is supposed to reflect and report on the changes in society. All in the media recognise that its thriving relies on people joining it from a range of backgrounds, bringing different experiences, opinions and interests to the job.

No would-be journalist should be put off by the make-up of the industry – or the image. Anyone who has ever been sufficiently interested to pick up a paper, listen to the radio news or watch a television bulletin and thought, I could do that, can have a go. Unlike medicine, law or accountancy, journalism doesn't require the highest academic qualifications and years of study. If you can do it, you are it.

But don't think that means it is going to be easy to get a job. Journalism is as difficult to join as the cream of the white-collar professions for a simple reason: there are many more people who want to be journalists than possibly ever could be. Each year tens of thousands of people express an interest in becoming a journalist. Many may be thinking of journalism only as a second or third career choice, but there are still plenty who have it at the top of their list but can't get in. Under a thousand people succeed each year.

So how do you become one of them? How do you set off on the path to being the next Trevor McDonald or Lynda Lee Potter? Sadly, there is no simple answer. There is no right way to get into journalism, no set career path and no inevitable reward of promotion to the pinnacle of the profession for serving your time.

But that means there is also no wrong way. You can decide it's the job for you long after your first careers night at school, after graduating from university or even after years working elsewhere. Another cliché about journalism, and without doubt the one with the firmest base in reality, is that there are as many ways into the profession as there are people in it. For example, among journalists working on national newspapers there is everything from an editor who was a trainee monk (Richard Addis, of the *Express*) to reporters who have been chefs or even pop stars – and that's just in the *Guardian*'s newsroom.

Of course, the majority of the estimated 100,000 or so people working in journalism or allied jobs have only ever worked in the one field. Most are now removed from the day-to-day comings and goings of a newsroom: there are no more than an estimated 15,000 news journalists. But in addition there are those who work in features, producing longer pieces less directly related to news or perhaps tangential to it, in sport or arts, or on the production side of journalism, designing newspapers or editing packages for broadcast. Others may have switched into public relations or management.

But almost all will have started from the same point as the

most wet-behind-the-ears trainee: wanting to be at the fore-front of what's going on, reporting the news. All learnt the basics of reporting before developing their skills and career. It is the route you will take.

THE JOB

It's all in the name, surely? A reporter reports. But news journalism also includes the executives who decide which stories to report, the subeditors who fit them into the paper or into broadcast packages and the editors who oversee the focus, content and tone of papers or programmes. Further variety comes from the range of topics which generate stories: general news, politics, business and sport, to name the main ones, each requiring reporters, news editors, subs and editors.

Common to the different types of news journalist and the three branches of the media – print, radio and television, although the Internet is rapidly joining them – is the set of attributes needed to do the job successfully: speed and accuracy in gathering the news and producing an easily understandable version of it for the public; coolness under pressure; and drive.

Perhaps you're not sure you have what it takes; journalism may seem a bit daunting as a career. The good news is that most of the skills are learnt. The overwhelming majority of journalists working at any of the higher levels of the profession have worked their way up from the very bottom. They did their stint on a local paper, often a small weekly, a community radio station or another form of grassroots reporting. They honed their interviewing and writing skills covering everything from golden weddings to charity fund-raising events, so that when the time came to cover bigger stories they knew exactly what they were looking for and what to do.

Generally, the local paper is the most common starting-point for any career. Radio stations regularly recruit reporters with newspaper experience and add the technical skills needed to operate and edit the audio equipment to the reporting nous which the journalists bring with them. Television stations are even more eager devourers of newspaper reporters, as they not only often take on the ex-print radio reporters but also recruit direct from newspapers. If you ever read profiles of big-name journalists, there is a good chance they started on papers such as the *Banbury Cake* or *Pulman's Weekly News*. And they never regret it.

The reason is simple: there is no better training ground. On a small paper there are no specialists, so everything is shared about. If that means you have to cover an agricultural show one week, it also means you will get the chance to cover the biggest stories – such as serious crimes, royal visits or major accidents and other breaking news – in subsequent weeks. You will be sent to cover court and council meetings, be asked to write features or opinion pieces as well as probably getting the chance to do some arts and sport reporting. You will get a good all-round grounding. And, not insignificantly, if you are learning the ropes and perhaps sometimes making mistakes, you will be in a small pond where the ripples you may inadvertently create will soon subside. Finally, there's a greater likelihood of someone having the time to take you to one side and help you.

QUALITIES AND REWARDS

There are certain qualities which editors look for in would-be reporters. You need to be:

- interested in current affairs, from politics at Westminster to the celebrity news. You would be of no use to a newspaper if you were sent to cover a politician's speech and couldn't spot the most interesting angle to report. Equally what use would you be to a news editor if he or she sent you to report on Ken Morley opening a supermarket and you knew nothing about his television role as *Coronation Street*'s Reg Holdsworth?

- curious about people, places and events. Journalism is all about people – what they do, when, where and why they do it and how it affects other people and society. The investigation of Fred West's activities in Gloucester was revealed by a reporter who wanted to know why police officers were digging at 25 Cromwell Street. If your first instinct is to say, 'It's none of my business,' how will you ever get a story?

◆ able to write. The language used to report the news is simple and clear because it has to be. Readers or listeners will not persevere if they do not understand a story. It is a journalist's job to gather the facts, sift them and present them in an easy-to-understand way – without spelling, grammar or punctuation mistakes

◆ flexible and capable of working under pressure. News happens twenty-four hours a day, 365 days a year, which means journalists have to work those hours. You will, at some time, have to work nights, weekends and bank holidays, even Christmas occasionally. Stories also break five minutes before deadlines. If you're asked to write one quickly, no one will be able to afford to have you cracking under the strain

◆ aware of the role the media fulfil and able to play a part in it. Every day millions of people demand to know what has happened – overseas, in Britain, in their county and town – and they rely on journalists to tell them equitably and accurately. To do so you have to be able to talk to Tories and represent their views justly even if you're a socialist, report on religious fanatics and their outlook even if you're an atheist, or give peace campaigners a fair platform even if your family is steeped in military history

◆ determined. The one quality needed above all others.

As job specifications go, it's a demanding one. But don't think the rewards alone will make it all worth while. Far from being the glamorous job often portrayed, journalism can be routine. It is generally not about mingling with exciting, famous or powerful people in fantastic surroundings. It is about sitting in council chambers or magistrates' courts, hanging on the telephone in the office or loitering outside someone's house to try to grab a word with them as they arrive or depart. For every opportunity to travel to a far-flung country, interview a top politician or meet a film star, there are thousands and thousands of two-sentence stories on petty crime or weather round-ups. You may never, in your entire career, even get the chance of a glittering assignment, so don't go into journalism if you just want the drama and excitement of overseas travel or hobnobbing. We can't all be Kate Adie, Jeremy Paxman or Andy Coulson. Nor may we want to be.

What's more, the pay is poor, particularly at entry levels. Some trainees earn under £7,000 per annum, according to the NUJ. It supports proposals for a minimum wage of £4.26 an hour and estimates that up to 20 per cent of provincial journalists would benefit from it. Two-fifths of the NUJ membership survey earned under £20,000, while fewer than four out of 100 earned more than £50,000.

Younger journalists earned the least, with more than 60 per cent of those under twenty-five being paid under £15,000. A fifth earned less than £10,000. In one case recently a reporter even resorted to cleaning the office in which she worked to bring in some extra money. The £17.50 a month helped boost her salary of £7,200 – but she had to provide her own vacuum cleaner.

Long hours, poor pay and demanding work. There can be, and is, only one result: stress. In a survey conducted via the *Guardian* the majority of thousands of media workers responding to a questionnaire reported they worked more than forty hours a week and a third earned under £19,000. But 94 per cent claimed to suffer from stress, 39 per cent frequently.

Even so, the pluses outweigh the minuses. Two-thirds of those stressed and underpaid respondents enjoyed their jobs. Even without the glamour factor, journalism can be a highly rewarding career, one in which you can go to work every day and not know what challenges may face you. You could be sent anywhere to report on interesting stories and meet fascinating people; you could discover a topic which might inspire you into further research and prompt a fruitful and fulfilling investigation; you will learn more about society and its workings, good and bad. If you are lucky, you might also enjoy a similar relationship with other countries – even if it is on a short trip which starts with a news editor asking the question all reporters want to hear: 'Have you got a passport?'

Overseas trips for home-based reporters generally fall into two categories. They are either assignments, firmly linked to a specific story, such as following an aid convoy, or 'freebies', trips organised by public relations officers (PRs) keen to promote something and willing to send you somewhere exotic to do it – for example, test driving a new car in the south of France or reporting the launch of a new tourism drive in South Africa. Such trips are the most obvious fringe benefit of being a journalist. But there are also complimentary tickets for concerts, films or other events, promotional copies of videos or music and free entry to sports fixtures, although all – well, most – are tied to work, either as reports or reviews. They are, simply, part of the job.

Travel can be more than just part of the job. News is not exclusive to this country. Britons want to know about what is happening elsewhere in the world and they need reporters to tell them about it. From a humble start on a small weekly paper you could easily end up overseas, working on reports on the biggest stories imaginable. More information about becoming a foreign correspondent or working abroad in other capacities is contained in Chapter 6. But for now it is enough to know that few people get foreign postings without learning the trade at home first.

THE WAY AHEAD

There are thousands of newspapers and radio and television stations offering openings for journalists, ranging from small weekly papers to such worldwide organisations as the BBC and the international press agency Reuters.

It is possible to get your first job in the vast majority of them: both the BBC and Reuters offer in-house training, as do many others of the biggest employers in the media, including, in a recent development, several national newspapers. However, the scramble for such places is the fiercest in an industry which is highly competitive at the best of times. Even if you want to break in at lower levels, it will be tough. You will certainly have to apply to more than one potential employer or training centre. If you get a choice of possible routes into your first job, you will be lucky; if you get even one, you will have done well; if you struggle at first, remember the most important qualification for journalism: determination. Try again.

As the media have expanded – first with radio, then television and now cutting-edge technology such as cable TV and the Internet – what was once a simple picture of entry into it and career development once in has become more complicated. The traditional first stop was a local paper, initially as a training ground, then less so as colleges began to teach the rudiments. Everyone would serve an apprenticeship on a small paper before moving on to bigger ones (shifting into management, production or even editing en route), perhaps even the nationals, or into radio and television. Nowadays there are college courses in radio and television and university degrees in journalism.

For most, though, a local paper will still be the entry point, not necessarily because it is the best way to start a career – although many will still say it is – but simply because it is the most likely. You can start off in radio or television, but the one attribute you will need as a journalist in all three media is a nose for news. Unlike tape editing or speaking to camera, it can't be easily taught. If you've got it, your career should be long and fruitful; if you haven't, you may struggle even to get started. And any editor looking for new recruits – be it for national newspapers, radio or television – will look at a candidate with experience on a local paper and know they have got that nose for news, no doubt honed during their early weeks, months and years in a real newsroom.

Therefore, local papers are the starting-point of this guide. Regional and national titles and broadcast journalism follow. But that does not mean that if you think you want to be the next Sue McGregor or Martyn Lewis, you should only read the section on radio or television. Tips on how to become a news journalist, a flavour of the job generally and the common pitfalls – all relevant across all branches of the media – are included in each chapter. Most of what is written about the news-gathering operation and office atmosphere, for example, applies universally. In any case, a good working knowledge of the media as a whole is an advantage for anyone who wants to work in a particular branch of it. You can make that decision once you know what to expect as a reporter – or in any of the alternative journalistic jobs – and what skills and qualifications different employers demand.

Aim high by all means, but don't neglect the basics. You may know a certain subject inside out and know major figures in it well, but if you can't write a story or, worse still, even spot one, you will never make it as any sort of journalist. You may want your career to be as memorable as the Goal of the Season, but footballers such as Eric Cantona and Alan Shearer learnt how to trap and pass the ball before anything else. If you think journalism is different and you can just breeze into the Premier League – or, conversely, that you'll be stuck in Division Three for ever if you don't start at the top – just look at the career of one young reporter who started on a college course and spent ten years on local weekly papers before trying to break into national newspapers. Just over ten years later the reporter in question, Phil Hall, was appointed to his current job as editor of the country's biggest-selling newspaper, the *News of the World*.

Another example is one of Britain's best-known broadcasters. John Humphrys, now of the *Today* programme, spent five years on a local weekly paper and a year on a daily before moving into commercial television as a scriptwriter. A switch to the BBC was the start of fifteen years of reporting, both at home and overseas, before swapping life on the road for the stability of studio-based presenting. His advice to aspiring journalists today is to get a degree and then do a postgraduate journalism course. 'Better still to get your knees brown on a local paper or radio station . . . but I would say that wouldn't I?' So would many others.

Breaking In

Out there, somewhere, is a job for you. It could be close to your home on a local paper – a weekly, most likely, of which there will be at least one near by. But wherever you live there will probably be an evening title, occasionally two or more, and perhaps a regional morning paper. There may even be the district office of a national title in the vicinity. There will also be at least one BBC and one commercial local radio station – and, again, possibly more than one of each. Finally, there will be two regional television stations, one BBC and one commercial, and perhaps even a cable channel. All of them need news; all need news journalists.

If you spread your net further afield and decide that you will go wherever the work is, the choice is multiplied many times over. Through natural wastage – retirements and people leaving the profession – there are hundreds, if not thousands, of openings each year. If you add in vacancies as a result of new launches and new formats – for example, satellite television and Channel Five – as well as trade magazines and jobs in PR and similar areas related to journalism, the potential choice is staggering. Eventually. First, though, you will have to get the basic qualifications and experience which will allow you to choose which path to pursue.

The plum jobs are often seen as those on the nationals – on papers or in broadcasting. A member of the public is perhaps more likely to be impressed, rightly or wrongly, when you say you work for the *Daily Mail* or the *Observer* rather than the *Oxford Mail* or the *Rochdale Observer*. Similarly ITN is likely to carry more kudos than Invicta FM. But, remember, there are as many fine journalists in the regions, working for local papers and broadcasters. Many ex-national journalists have gone back to their regional roots and many of their colleagues there could have thrived on the nationals but chose not to.

Because the jobs at the top are often seen as the best, they are also the most sought-after. As a newcomer, you are more likely to start lower down the ladder, often on the bottom rung. And that means the suburbs of Oxford or Rochdale rather than Fleet Street. But don't think that means it will necessarily be easier to get a foot in the door. There are far fewer vacancies than wannabe journalists, whatever level you enter the industry.

THE EMPLOYERS

There are approximately 1,500 local newspaper titles in the country. They range from the famous regional titles, such as the *Yorkshire Post*, and big-selling, big-city evenings such as Wolverhampton's *Express and Star* – which sells up to 215,000 copies, only about 50,000 less than the *Independent* – to a plethora of small freesheets.

Just like the national titles you are likely to be familiar with, local and regional papers can be brash tabloids, modelled on the *Sun*, or considered broadsheets with heavyweight columnists and teams of specialist writers like those of *The Times*, the *Telegraph* or the *Guardian*. Only a generation ago many provincial papers were broadsheets, but now most are tabloid, although in the mid-market *Express/Daily Mail* mould rather than the full-on soar-away, sensation-seeking style of the *Sun*, *Mirror* or *Daily Star*.

Also like the nationals, most local and regional titles are part of groups of papers owned by large competing companies. While you will no doubt have heard of Rupert Murdoch, owner of 35 per cent of the national press via News International, and the Mirror Group, you may not know of Newsquest, Northcliffe (the regional arm of the Mail Group) or Trinity, the big players in the provinces. Each owns between 11 and 12 per cent of the regional press. Then comes

United Provincial Newspapers (the Express Group's equivalent of Northcliffe), with around 6 per cent, and Johnston Press which spent £231 million in 1995/6 to acquire seventy-six titles. Even so it owns only about 4 per cent of the market. To many in the media themselves some of these names are unfamiliar, partly because the ultimate owner of a paper may be of less importance than its local management or editor and partly because three of the top five are relative newcomers. Like Johnston, both Trinity and Newsquest were little-known until they bought titles.

All of this may seem of little relevance to would-be journalists, except that it proves that one of the most commonly repeated theories about provincial press journalism is doubted by some astute, powerful and obviously wealthy business figures who should know what they are talking about. That theory holds that the local newspaper industry is a 'mature' business which is now locked into unrelenting decline. But the investment by Johnston, Trinity and Newsquest, among others, shows there is thought to be life in the papers yet.

Admittedly, the critics have some decent ammunition. Circulation of the regional press has been in steady decline for decades. In the past fifteen years alone 300 weekly papers and eight dailies have closed as circulation has plummeted. To take one extreme but by no means unique example, the *Brighton Evening Argus* sold 111,000 copies a night in 1975; twenty-one years later it was selling under 55,000. Every time the Audit Bureau of Circulations, the official sales-monitoring organisation, publishes its latest lists there are plenty of editors with disquieting figures to mull over. In the January–June 1996 period only twenty-two of the ninety-seven biggest titles put on sales.

But still they sold more than 5 million copies each day. According to the Newspaper Society, the association representing local press owners, such sales translate into 4,000 local papers being sold in Britain every minute. They also account for more of the total advertising market than the national titles. With new design and developments such as the introduction of full colour and an increased demand for, and ability to supply, the most local of local news, there are improvements which will keep local papers alive for some time yet. Readers still want the latest news. And that means reporters will still be needed to write it.

COURSES AND QUALIFICATIONS

Jobs are sometimes advertised. A local paper may occasionally carry a small advertisement saying 'Trainee reporter wanted', which could be your chance. Alternatively the weekly trade magazine covering news about journalism, *Press Gazette*, has several pages of career openings at the back of each issue. The *Guardian*'s media section, on Mondays, has even more advertisements.

But ninety-nine per cent of these jobs require experience. Many advertisements include the discouraging but under-standable phrase 'Sorry, no beginners'. And advertisements saying 'Wanted: new recruits' are near to non-existent. The reason is simple: editors do not need to advertise for new blood.

Unsolicited applications from hopefuls arrive on a regular basis and are filed away for future reference. School pupils and students who impress on work experience can be offered a traineeship. Editors who still struggle to find applicants through either of these ways have a final trick up their sleeves: calling one of the colleges churning out reporters already trained in the basics and desperate to apply the theory to real stories.

The budding reporters emerging from these colleges have followed one of two ways into print journalism: 'pre-entry'. The alternative is known as 'direct entry'. The difference is broadly that in the former you attend college before getting a job, while in the latter you get the job first. Two similar routes exist for broadcast journalism, although not under the same names. All journalists, in news at least, follow one of the routes: it is almost unheard of for a news reporter not to be trained.

Common to all routes are the absolute minimum educa-tional standards asked of would-be journalists. You must have passed at least five GCSEs, or equivalents, at grades A to C.

One must be in English. Very occasionally, if a candidate shows exceptional talent or the promise of it, the qualification criteria are lowered. But, if anything, the standards are generally above the minimum: most colleges will require at least two A-levels or an equivalent qualification. Even then, most students are further qualified: around half of them now are graduates.

Research published by the London College of Printing reported that six times as many aspiring journalists today have degrees compared to the 7.5 per cent who did forty years ago. Another survey, in the *Guardian*, discovered that 57 per cent of those working in the media, including advertising and magazines, had degrees (and almost half were aged under thirty-one). On some contemporary training courses graduates make up anything up to 80 per cent of the intake; the figure is even higher for wannabe broadcasters, for whom it is as good as mandatory to have a degree. There are many courses for print journalism which are now purely, and deliberately, aimed at postgraduates.

The rise in educational standards applies across the board. In the 1950s a quarter of journalists had no secondary-education qualification; now it is only 4 per cent. But those without formal qualifications, or older applicants, should not be deterred. Editors are often keen to take on older reporters for two reasons: first, they have a more settled lifestyle and will not be looking to spend eighteen months on a paper before moving on; second, they often have strong local knowledge and contacts in many areas, both geographical and social, while younger applicants do not. To provide a route into journalism for such candidates year-long access courses are run at five colleges (listed in Appendix B). Once these are completed, successful students can apply for a place on one of the full-time journalism courses.

There is a final piece of good news for the over-thirties: you can take a little less notice of the intricacies of the formal training structure (at least as operated by the NCTJ – see below), as it is often modified for older applicants. You will most likely still have to undergo the same training and achieve the same standards, but there is a little more flexibility for you and your editor to arrange the details of it. That, as you will see, can make things an awful lot easier.

PRE-ENTRY

The pre-entry route only involves editors, overtly, at its climax – when it's time to apply for jobs. Instead the central role is taken by the National Council for the Training of Journalists (NCTJ), which has overseen the education of journalists for more than forty years. Based in Harlow, Essex, it runs courses, supervises and accredits others and awards a final diploma, the National Certificate, to mark the successful completion of a journalist's training.

Each year in the region of 20,000 hopefuls make enquiries to the NCTJ (see Appendix B for the address) about a career in journalism. A couple of thousand go on to complete an application form. They are trying to win a place on one of the twenty or so one-year, full-time courses or one of the shorter ones run purely for postgraduates. Those thought to be suitable candidates are invited to take a written test at one of the regional centres. If they pass, they are invited for an interview which acts as the final hurdle in a demanding selection process. About 500 students each year win a place.

On any course you will be taught the rudiments of reporting: how to structure a story, how to turn a press release or speech into a news item, how to gather and collate the facts on an assignment. You will also learn about local government (councils and local taxation) and central government (Parliament and the Cabinet), as well as newspaper law (including the exact definitions of the dreaded word 'libel') and shorthand. This last skill is perhaps the most important. Can you imagine having to ask the Prime Minister, or even a local councillor, to repeat an answer to a question because you didn't manage to write it down the first time?

At the end of the course you will take preliminary exams. You will need to pass all subjects and be capable of 100-words-per-minute shorthand. A very few editors may be willing to give some leeway and allow you to retake any papers you failed once you have started work, but most will insist on a full set of passes. And in a climate where the supply of would-be new reporters exceeds demand, they can afford to insist.

The search for an employer will begin with *Press Gazette* and the *Media Guardian*, the college noticeboard (where many newspapers post their latest new vacancies) and probably a copy of one of the reference books (listed in Appendix A) to get names and addresses for those speculative letters to editors which often bring results. Be prepared for plenty of letter writing – and many rejection letters. Your determination will be put to the test again.

When you get a job – and the success rate claimed for NCTJ pre-entry courses is close to 100 per cent – you will be allowed to move towards the next step in your training: the National Certificate Examination (NCE – described in detail below), which is the final exam taken after a period of between eighteen months' and two years' experience. You will start work as a junior reporter, or trainee, and only become a 'senior' after passing the NCE.

A tiny minority of editors do not care about the exam, arguing that if you can do the job, you do not need a piece of paper to prove it. They may also shrug if you fail some of your preliminary exams. However, if you never formally pass your training, you may find that the next newspaper to which you apply demands such pieces of paper and therefore rejects you. Just because a minority of editors ignore training structures doesn't mean they all will. Furthermore, there is a financial angle: most employers will pay a senior salary only to a recognised senior journalist – that is, one who has passed the NCE.

One note of caution about training courses concerns money. NCTJ courses do not attract mandatory grants. Local education authorities decide if journalism students qualify for support – and most do not. Wisely, the NCTJ stresses that before anyone even applies for a place on a course, they should check exactly what the financial situation will be. The absence of a grant does not mean you have to miss out on a course as long as you can pay the fees, of between £3,000 and £4,000, and live by other means. That usually means a loan or parental support. Some bursaries are available: the NUJ supports some candidates from ethnic minorities (the scheme is described in further detail in Chapter 2) and some newspapers do sponsor students at the most prestigious colleges: City University, London, and the University of Wales in Cardiff. But it remains a sad fact that the overwhelming majority of students have to pay their own way.

Those two colleges can legitimately claim to be described as the Oxbridge of journalism training: they offer the élite courses. Tutors at City boast that half of the students from its postgraduate newspaper course find their first jobs on national titles. Graduates from the equivalent course in Cardiff do not have such immediate success, mostly joining regional papers initially. But many of them also end up on the nationals.

Getting your first job on a national or even a large regional paper, though, could have disadvantages as well as the obvious advantages of kudos and achievement. You may suffer in terms of formal training, which might matter if you struggle to make the grade; or lack an all-round grounding covering the basics, from agricultural shows to Crown court. Of course, it could be argued, such problems might be nice ones to have. But do not think that just because you don't attend the premier colleges and land your first job at a high level you cannot progress. There are many national journalists – if that's what you want to be and, again, not everyone does – who attended a standard NCTJ college. Some perhaps didn't even participate in the formal training system at all.

In journalism you are as good as your cuttings book – and if you can compile a good one and show determination, you can go as far as any graduate of Oxbridge, its journalistic equivalent or both.

DIRECT ENTRY

The alternative to pre-entry is direct entry. Instead of going to college and then getting a job, you do it the other way around. Getting addresses from reference books, you will have to write to editors hoping to impress one enough to offer you a traineeship. When you start work you will be sent a distance-learning pack from the NCTJ to help you pick up the most basic of the basics. After a probationary period of about six months and a pre-preliminary exam, your paper will send you, on 'block release' for about three months, to one of the NCTJ colleges. You will learn the same range of writing and other skills as pre-entry students and sit the same preliminary exams. You then return to your paper to work your way towards the NCE, again after about eighteen months. More than 100 people a year follow the NCTJ direct-entry route into journalism.

The main advantage of direct entry is financial. Not only will you be paid, however little, both before you go to college and while you are there, but you will also avoid having to pay the fees for your course: they will be met by your employer. And, given that grants for journalism courses are a rarity, you will be thousands of pounds better off than many pre-entry students. The second advantage is security: once you have your job, you do not need to worry. You will not be in the position of pre-entry students who have to compete against their classmates and, as many pre-entry courses finish at a similar time, against students from other colleges too for whatever jobs are going.

The financial burden borne by many pre-entry students has led to criticism of the entire NCTJ system. Many editors and proprietors have voiced concern about the inevitable result: the gentrification of journalism. Nowadays those who can afford the costs, or whose parents can, are among the most common entrants into the profession. Aspiring reporters from less affluent backgrounds who cannot foot the bill are excluded. The result? 'Middle-class twenty-somethings', as one paper dubbed them, flooding into journalism.

The trend has been exaggerated by the increasing desire of graduates, often from more well-to-do backgrounds, to become journalists. Young reporters with degree-level knowledge of politics or literature are joining papers expecting to write about issues or do major interviews, whereas in fact they are being asked to go out to council estates or tower blocks and find stories strong on human interest – that is, about people and their lives – or chase fire engines en route to emergencies.

Too many are thought to want to write only considered pieces for the national broadsheets without getting their hands inky at lower levels of the media. Significant numbers of executives, both in the newspaper industry and increasingly in broadcasting, have become unhappy with the result: trainees who often have no empathy with the people on whom they are reporting, no feel for the readers, listeners or viewers and their lives and, worse still, no desire to cultivate these facets.

Then there is the third factor adding to the tarnished reputation of the NCTJ: concern about the peculiar animal which is the NCE. It is designed to test the skills you will bring to a story. Typically it will involve having to interview a senior policeman about an incident before writing a story from the facts you have uncovered. Other strands will test your ability to write similarly accurate stories from a speech and a handout not dissimilar to a press release.

However, it is all fake. The policeman is really a NCTJ official, as is the speaker. The exam takes place at an NCTJ centre, not at the scene of an accident or in a real newsroom. As you cannot schedule real car crashes or muggings to coincide with exams or ask the Prince of Wales to pop down to college to give a speech, the tests are artificial – though as realistic a recreation of the type of story you will have to cover as is possible. Some critics ask why someone who has been working as a journalist with no problems for two years should suddenly find they are not good enough for senior status because of a one-day test; the system's defenders counter-claim that if a trainee cannot stand the pressure of a mocked-up newsroom situation, what chance have they got in the real thing?

Even what is tested and taught by the NCTJ has come under fire. In the forty years since it began its training system, newspapers have undergone revolutionary changes. Its critics say it has not followed suit. Why, they say, teach shorthand when portable tape recorders are cheap and easy to use? (An easy point to refute, as tape recorders are never allowed into any court, one of the regular sources of stories.) But other criticisms, such as the lack of any education about the commercial side of newspapers (i.e., advertising and circulation), are more justified. Today's journalists need to be better equipped than those of forty years ago, just as modern cars boast more basic features than post-war ones. Young reporters today will need to be computer-literate, *au fait* with the production and commercial side of newspapers and perhaps even trained to take photographs.

Given the litany of complaints, you will not be surprised to hear that some editors and proprietors have revolted.

MODERN APPRENTICESHIPS, NVQs AND IN-HOUSE TRAINING

In the last couple of years some editors have started deliberately turning away from successful pre-entry students and have tried to unearth rawer, more local talent. A new type of training – the modern apprenticeship – has developed, aimed at school leavers. Participants are aged between sixteen and twenty-three (so can, in theory, include graduates). They do not follow the NCTJ route but are trained with the aim of attaining a National Vocational Qualification (NVQ), a general vocational benchmark introduced by the government in 1992, or the Scottish SVQ, both recognised as being the equivalent of the NCE. The chief differences between them and the NCTJ system is that there is no period at college, just structured learning on the job, and a system of continual assessment rather than exams.

With funding available from government-backed local training agencies, modern apprenticeships have the extra benefit of saving employers money. Each trainee attracts around £6,000 of funding. But the scheme's emergence is as much to do with genuine concern over the make-up of those entering journalism as hard cash. Richard Beamish, head of training at the Newspaper Society, acknowledges the problem: 'We are losing talented people and we are not getting a proper cross-section of society in journalism. It's become only those who can afford it, or whose parents can, or those who are prepared to go further into debt who go on training courses.'

With employers expressing such concerns, it seems modern apprenticeships will become more and more common. Indeed, thirteen publishing groups have already launched schemes, most in the last six months of 1996. In fact, despite the name and their newness, they are actually a return to the past, when the main route into journalism was via your local paper. As many editors and executives have followed that route, it's doubly certain they will back its re-introduction. The practice may even start to appear in the broadcast sector.

Cumbrian Newspapers, a small independent group with two daily titles and a handful of weeklies, was one of the first to introduce a modern apprenticeship scheme. About half a dozen teenagers have been recruited each year since its inception, not through colleges or advertisements in *Press Gazette* or the *Guardian* but through small notices carried in the group's own titles. Its younger readers are becoming its reporters. Robin Burgess of the group says, 'We wanted to employ local people who would have an empathy with the community they serve and are interested in it. There have been some concerns within the industry about the NCTJ and its slightly rigid approach, but we don't necessarily have a problem with that – and some of our journalists are doing the NCE as well as an NVQ. We just wanted to get a better nucleus of local journalists.'

Modern apprenticeships, however, are just the latest reaction to a decade-old discontent with the NCTJ and its perceived faults. An earlier result was the development of in-house schemes. In the mid-1980s, in the first reaction against the NCTJ, some of the larger newspaper groups broke away to establish their own training schemes. Westminster Press was the first, in 1987, followed by Thomson and several others. Trainees learnt the same basics, but often with other aspects of the job thrown in as well – perhaps production skills or a dissertation on media-related issues. The learning environment was, and is, different too: far more akin to a newsroom than a college with, for example, set hours.

In the past couple of years, as the ownership of such groups has fluctuated and the desire to run expensive centres died, most have closed. Now there are only three: Trinity's, the Midland News Association's and what was Westminster Press's. A fourth group, United, runs an in-house training scheme but generally recruits students to it from standard pre-entry courses (and sponsors students at several).

More details about each are given in Appendix B, but it is worth looking more closely at the biggest – the Editorial Centre in Hastings, which used to be Westminster Press's centre – to appreciate the differences between the NCTJ route and in-house training. For a start the courses, run twice a year, are shorter: fifteen weeks as opposed to a year. But they are still pre-entry. What sets them apart from NCTJ ones – and takes them closer to direct entry, in fact – is that most of the students on them are sponsored by employers, who then generally offer jobs to those who pass their exams. Among the employers who sponsor students at Hastings are the *Financial Times*, Newsquest, Southern Newspapers and Eastern Counties Newspapers (the last three of whom all used to have their own training centres). And, in passing, it is worth noting those students are not all twenty-somethings. Recent trainees have included a barrister and an Army captain, both aged thirty-six, a travel agent aged thirty-one, and a photographer aged fifty-one.

To win a place at an in-house centre you will have to follow the direct-entry route: impressing an editor and getting a job or sponsorship before starting your formal training. All the in-house centres also offer pre-entry openings for self-financing students, but anyone considering such a move will have to be able to afford the fees of up to £4,000 – and to support themselves. However, if you successfully complete a course, you will have a qualification which is as close to a guarantee of employment as possible. The money would be a good investment – if you are certain journalism is for you and you have the cash available in the first place.

In-house schemes train approximately another 120 new entrants to journalism each year. Some issue their own diplomas, based on continuous assessment, others adhere to the NVQ approach and a few offer both. Only one, the Midland News Association, is accredited by the NCTJ. But you should not worry too much about which qualification you obtain, as they are generally regarded as being similar. As long as you have the basics, editors who might hire you in the future are far more likely to go on a strong set of cuttings and a good interview.

Richard Beamish says employers will look at National Certificates, NVQs and in-house diplomas as equivalents. 'We regard them all as being very similar. If it's good training, it's good training no matter what qualification comes at the end of it.' But the system is ripe for reform, and the Guild of Editors, the forum of editors and training directors, is aiming for this. It has suggested a new system of training, essentially marrying the best of the NCTJ and NVQ approaches in a bid to move back to a position where there is one recognised national training qualification.

It would be a three-stage diploma, according to proposals now under discussion. It is suggested only 'high fliers' would take all three stages, the last one being more specialist, with reporters who were happy to remain at a lower level not taught this stage. Training would also include far more about advertising and production as part of an ethos of multi-skilling.

Until that unified qualification is launched – it is well worth keeping abreast of developments via *Press Gazette* – and the training system is simplified, you will have to be careful to check exactly what training is on offer. Some papers pay lip service to training but then begrudge their new reporters taking time to complete modules or continuous-assessment tasks. Some might throw you into your job and never offer advice or guidance as you work towards the NCE or similar qualification. Remember that you should be the one most interested in your training. It will be up to you to check that all the basic areas of work – from court reporting to crime calls – are covered. If in doubt, the NCTJ or the NUJ may be able to help you.

DEGREES: MEDIA STUDIES AND JOURNALISM

At the same time as the fragmentation of the training system, there has been a second trend complicating matters further still: the development of the media as an academic topic.

The NCTJ and subsequent courses devised in reaction to it had one thing in common: they were vocational. They were about taking raw recruits and producing at least half-finished journalists who had the tools – shorthand, knowledge of law and local government as well as writing skills – needed in a newsroom. Any editor hiring a junior reporter from a training college, or sending a trainee to one, would be confident that the new hand could be dispatched, on his or her first day, to a court case or council meeting and know what to do.

But the academic rigours brought to journalism meant students began to analyse the media rather than practising how to be part of them. Media studies, as the new field became known, did not pretend to be vocational. Graduates might be able to discuss the historical development or political slant of the press, or other topics, but nothing remotely relevant to getting them a job in journalism. Aside from what many journalists saw – and still see – as its pointlessness, media studies also disconcerted them, as all of a sudden they found they had gone from reporting to being reported on. As one insider puts it, 'The hostility towards media studies is like the hostility juvenile delinquents have towards social workers.'

Whatever the cause, the level of hostility is massive. It is perhaps best illustrated by an article in the *Independent* in the autumn of 1996. Headlined 'How not to be a journalist', it is worth reproducing in full to appreciate the vitriol:

Media studies is a trivial, minor field of research, spuriously created for jargon-spinners and academic makeweights. Students learn nothing of value because the subject doesn't know its own purpose, is unimportant and because most people teaching it don't know what they're talking about. Yet it is the fastest-growing subject in higher education.

Careers counsellors might wonder why they have failed to stop students applying to waste their time and taxpayers' money. Perhaps we can help: this paper regards a degree in media studies as a disqualification for the career of journalism. That might put a few of them off.

Wishful thinking perhaps and to be qualified in two ways. First, some media studies courses are better than others. Some have a high practical content, allowing much hands-on work. Second, a degree is a degree and that's what many trainee journalists have to have today. Even if a media studies course is not practical, there may be a student newspaper or radio station where you could practise real skills. Editors are also unlikely to turn down promising recruits purely because they are media studies graduates. On the other hand, don't think a media studies degree will automatically help you on your way to becoming a journalist any more than one in sociology or plant sciences. You may even find it more difficult to get a foot in the door because you will have to overcome the hostility the subject provokes.

In the end, armed with a healthy amount of scepticism, you will have to look closely at the syllabus of any course and ask exactly what skills it will give you. If you would be no better off by doing such a course than if you did politics or English, do politics or English or something else. If you insist on doing a media studies course, make sure it is as practical as possible – and that you can defend it and yourself if an editor calls you for an interview.

A far more positive degree subject which has had an even more recent birth than media studies is journalism. The first course began in 1993 – a very tardy development, given that American universities have run such degrees for years. Now there are more than half a dozen, almost exclusively at the newer universities such as Central Lancashire and Teesside as well as City University, London, and University College, Cardiff.

In crucial ways these courses are far removed from media studies, although in many areas there is overlap as well. Many are accredited by the NCTJ, so you will study shorthand, law, local and central government as well as journalism to its pre-entry standards. You will therefore be as well placed to secure a post as a junior reporter as any other NCTJ-trained candidate. In some ways you will have more to offer, as you will also have studied the history of the press, marketing and even production techniques. Most of the courses offer students the chance to learn broadcasting skills, a useful added ingredient which may hold graduates in good stead in their later careers. Some can be taken with subsidiary subjects, giving a student a base in a more traditional subject such as economics, English or a modern language.

Again, the key is deciding what you want from a course and checking carefully to find one which fits your needs. The phrase which should be at the forefront of your mind all the time is: 'Buyer, beware.'

PHOTOGRAPHY AND BROADCASTING

In their heart of hearts, reporters know that the adage that a good picture is worth a thousand words is true. No matter how evocative the prose, no matter how emotional the story, a photograph which reinforces the facts by distilling them in a moving image – or, in the case of television, moving images – is what the general public remembers. The examples are numerous, but one of the most vivid, if a slightly aged picture today, was when the shattered nose cone of the bombed jumbo jet which crashed on Lockerbie was captured lying, detached from what was left of the rest of the plane, in a field.

It takes not only great technical ability to capture the instant history which most pictures are but also journalistic nous. Photographers have to be equally adept at the mechanics of setting up their pictures and the skill of conveying a story in such pictures. As with reporting, there are courses which teach the basics (although, like reporters, the best practitioners are often those who know the rules, then break them occasionally) of being a photojournalist (a reporter who also takes pictures) or a photographer alone. On top of the qualities needed for a reporter, photographers must have an eye which can see a different or better visual angle than the obvious one and then capture it on film.

Photographers and photojournalists enter the profession in the same way as reporters: via the NCTJ or an in-house scheme, direct or pre-entry. The qualifications needed are the same/similar: five GCSEs or equivalent, including English, for the former; an A-level in place of one GCSE for the latter. Alternatively, those without the relevant qualifications are eligible to apply for a place if they have had at least two years' experience of photography (inside or outside journalism) or have completed a further education course in photography.

The only difference to speak of between reporting and photography courses is that there is only one NCTJ college, in Sheffield, offering photography. The London College of Printing offers nightschool classes, while some universities and other colleges are now also offering photojournalism courses. But remember: buyer, beware.

Finally, a word about television and radio. In the past decade or so many courses have been established to train students specifically for radio and television. Many offer the hands-on experience of modern technical equipment which is a passport to a job. As a result an increasing number of entrants into broadcasting are graduates of these courses rather than veterans of papers. There is much to recommend the courses; they will be dealt with in Chapter 5.

GETTING THE EDGE

INTERVIEWS

Thousands of other people are reading this book or finding out the information in it from other sources. They all want to be journalists. They all want an editor or college tutor to pick them as one of the lucky ones who get the chance to become a reporter. The crunch question is how do you convince them to pick you?

Obviously there are no surefire ways, but there are certain things which are going to look impressive on your curriculum vitae (CV) or in the flesh at an interview. It should go without saying these are on top of the attributes described in the last section. An editor is hardly going to be impressed by someone who turns up late for the interview, blushes and becomes flustered at the first question and says, 'I don't really know,' when asked why he or she wants to be a journalist. You are going to have to be determined and as single-minded as if you were chasing the Watergate story. Your editor or tutor will want to see how resolute you can be.

First, of course, you have to get to the interview stage. When you are writing to editors or tutors you need to sell yourself. And, as you are hoping to become a professional writer, you need to compose your letter well or make sure your application form is clear and concise. A letter should have a snappy opening, a well-structured body of text and a clear explanation of your strengths and determination; an application form succinct points, well written. In both, above all make sure there are no spelling or grammatical errors. Show friends or parents your efforts and see if they spot any mistakes you might have missed. One 'it's' when you mean 'its' and your letter will probably be going the same place as your career: the bin.

With your letter should be a CV. It does not need to be long and detailed, but it needs to focus on every relevant detail, just like an application form. If you wrote for your school magazine, mention it; if you have done any media-related work experience, mention it; if you won a prize for English or if you have done a pre-entry course at journalism college, mention it. Most important, if you have cuttings of any stories you have had published which you feel will help you, attach a selection of them, but don't include one where you have misspelt a word in the first paragraph or with which you are unhappy. If you have cuttings from a range of publications, choose the ones from the biggest – the evening newspaper rather than the school magazine, the weekly paper rather than the fanzine.

With luck, and most likely after dozens of applications, you should get an interview. Applicants for jobs in other professions may be able to hone their interview skills as they undergo first and second interviews for a series of companies, but in journalism there is little chance of scores of interviews: you will probably be interviewed only once by a prospective editor or tutor and perhaps at most half a dozen times for different papers or courses. The golden rule is therefore: be prepared.

Make sure you have replies ready for the obvious questions like why you want to be a journalist, why you should be recruited over other applicants and why you want to join that particular paper or course. Brush up on the locality so that if, for example, one of its MPs was in the news the week before your visit, you know about the story and can talk about it. See if you can discover if there are any on-going stories – a fight to save a huge local factory perhaps – so you can drop it into conversation. Most important, check out the paper: buy the day's or week's copy before you arrive for your interview (editors will be impressed to see a copy of their paper tucked under your arm; tutors likewise, but for less personal reasons) and see if you can get hold of back issues. Perhaps arrive early for your interview, head for the local library and read its back copies of the paper. If your early arrival means you spot a story waiting to be done, then so much the better.

You will also have to be armed with some questions. Be wary, however, of asking things such as 'What are the hours?', as they imply you could be a clock-watcher. Pay and holiday allocation will probably have to be broached, but ensure you do not come across as someone after a job, any job, rather than a foothold in the only career you want. Keep such questions for the end of your interview when, if you feel it has gone well and you would like to work for the paper, you can ask them along with questions about training structure and promotion prospects. For your initial questions it is better to stick to probing about the paper and its future direction and to assessing how the editor works and his or her attitude to trainees and training.

WORK EXPERIENCE

To those wondering about cuttings and how to get them the answer most often lies in work experience. You can also have stories or interviews published if you submit them on a speculative basis to a title which you think might use them. For example, if a famous figure – a politician, pop star or Olympic athlete – visits your home town and you don't think anyone from the local paper or a specialist magazine will be able to cover it, why not go along and see if you can get an interview and write a piece from it? Check with the publication you are thinking of offering it to first, though. They can only say no. And if they say yes, you could have a story to write. More realistically, you might have heard about a snippet of news – perhaps a drugs scandal at a local school or a campaign to save a beauty spot – and write a report about it for a paper (or ring and tell them about it). Radio and television also thrive on such tip-offs. Remember you don't need a badge saying 'Journalist' to start spotting stories and offering them to newsdesks.

Another way of accumulating cuttings is via student newspapers. Many universities and colleges produce papers – some official, some not; some considerably better than others. A portfolio of pieces – or pictures, if you are a budding photographer – will always add weight to an application. The work itself may be a long way from what a 'real' paper produces, but at least it shows you were keen enough to get up and start off as a journalist.

But work experience is usually the most valuable – possibly providing cuttings, but from a profession publication. Media organisations are always looking for willing volunteers to help them out and potential new talent to unearth. You should get some idea of what the job entails by shadowing reporters as they go about their work and also get the chance to write some stories, even if they are News in Briefs, or Nibs. If you can take in a story which you think the paper might be interested in, you will immediately stand out from the pack of work-experience placements (many of whom are only in the office at the behest of their schools and spend every day looking as if they wished they were somewhere else). The editor might notice your contribution and ask his reporting team about you; if they respond favourably and there is an opening, you might even be one of the tiny minority who land a job from a week's unpaid effort.

On the other hand, work experience can be very unfulfilling and downright exploitative. The increased number of papers and broadcasters in recent years has provided welcome new opportunities for those wanting to break into journalism, but it also means there are many newsrooms being run on exceedingly tight budgets. Some executives under financial pressure see work experience as a source of free labour. That means they will string you along with the carrot of a job *eventually* dangled in front of your face. If you are on work experience for more than a limited period, perhaps a maximum of a month, you should really be paid in some way: per word written, on an expenses-only basis or at a day rate. If your 'employer' balks at such a suggestion, it might be best to leave.

The less serious, but equally dangerous, pitfall of work experience is that it can be frustrating and worthless if you are not given the chance to try your hand at reporting or at least to get a flavour of the job from accompanying the reporters on assignment. There is nothing worse than being stuck in the newsroom, watching and wanting to contribute but only being asked to make the tea. If this happens, approach whoever is responsible for you at the paper and ask them for something to do. Unfortunately, if they ignore your requests, there is little you can do except perhaps tell your careers adviser or teacher, who might allow you to cut short the placement, contact the editor to complain or even warn other aspiring journalists away from the employer.

But the best way of avoiding such a fate is probably, for the only time in your journalistic career, to aim low. Try to get a placement on a smaller paper. Staff there will value you far more than those in a vast newsroom where the executives are too busy to talk to you and the reporters are so numerous you struggle to find a regular point of contact. On bigger publications you might end up being sent out on the lunchtime sandwich run or, as happened in one case, being asked to do just one thing: pick up the editor's dry cleaning. The whole point of work experience is to get cuttings. From that point of view an afternoon at a weekly paper in which you have a story published is infinitely more worth while than a month doing nothing practical in the office of a national or regional.

Peter Sands, aged forty-one, is the head of the Editorial Centre, Hastings, the largest independent in-house training centre.

A humanities graduate, he began his career on a weekly paper in the north-east before moving to the region's morning, the *Northern Echo*, in 1979 and, later, to its sister evening title. He returned to the *Echo* as night editor and deputy editor before becoming its editor at the age of thirty-four.

The standards required to get into journalism these days are very, very high. We don't entertain anyone who has not shown a huge enthusiasm for journalism. The number of applicants who contact us every year is in the thousands and the successful ones clearly have to raise themselves above the rest.

I'm looking for people who have demonstrated that they can write and have been prepared to collect a portfolio of meaningful cuttings – we don't take on anyone who has not done some time on a newspaper. If they haven't enough experience, we advise them to go away and get some.

When they are interviewed, we are looking for people with personal confidence who can talk about themselves and the industry. We also test them for spelling and ask them to write a story from memory about something in the news at the time, to check they keep up with the news, and give them a passage to turn into a news story.

It used to be there were about 800 people a year recruited to the [newspaper] industry but now it's more like 500. All of those 500 are talented and bright, most of them graduates. They are recruited for their potential to be editors and they would all make editors. But that's a problem: the industry doesn't need 500 editors. We want people who are going to be very good district reporters, who maybe have an affinity with the people and places they serve. In the old days you had reporters who would stay in the same office at the same paper for years. That doesn't happen any more and some editors certainly believe they should be recruiting more people locally who might stay.

Because of the changes in the industry and in training, there is a lot of turmoil at the moment for somebody coming into journalism. It was hard when I joined my first paper, but it is harder now. I remember applying for lots of jobs – and getting lots of 'Dear John' letters. Now I tell trainees that for every one of them here, there are 150 others who want to be here. They are the lucky ones.

First Impressions

If you want to go into journalism entirely because you have been seduced by the image of the raincoat-wearing, go-getting reporter constantly meeting top-level contacts – insiders with information to offer – forget it. The majority of journalists, especially ones working in print, are office-based; even those who do get out regularly spend much of their time behind a VDU. On a bad day a journalist's itinerary can revolve more around trips to the coffee machine and the sandwich shop than anything further afield. Broadcasters, of course, have to go out of the office more: you can't record an interview or film over the telephone or from a press release.

But what else will working as a news journalist involve? The first thing to understand, before going into the details of the working day, is the structure of the newsroom.

THE NEWSROOM

This will be similar be it at a national television station or a weekly paper. Its most numerous occupants, gathering and writing the news, are the reporters. On a weekly paper there might be only two or three, on a national title two dozen or more. Each should have their own desk, with a telephone and a pile of paper, notepads and books which will contain reference material, vital telephone contact numbers and a collection of past and present stories.

The overwhelming majority will have a computer sitting in the prime position. Typewriters are rarely still used – although they were reasonably common until less than a decade ago –

and the days of carbon paper having to be pressed between two folios of writing paper to produce a 'black' (a copy of your story for your reference after the original has been used in the production process) are gone.

The switch to new technology has revolutionised newsrooms. Gone is the rattle of dozens of typewriter keys being struck, the din as orders were barked above the racket and the acres of paper generated by blacks, top copies and discarded stories; in have come humming VDUs, electronic message systems and computer disks. Also gone are the printers who once typeset the stories for printing. With them in many offices, as pages are sent down computer lines to distant printers, have gone the vibrations which began when the presses started to roll. Indeed, many offices themselves have disappeared, or at least been gutted beyond recognition, to be replaced by new premises on industrial estates, renovated buildings or, in the case of the seven national titles based in Canary Wharf, a new tower block. The trend may have been less pronounced in the regions, but it still exists.

Despite these changes in environment, the structure inside remains largely the same as it has been for decades. Reporters from years ago might not know how to use the technology of today's journalism, but they would recognise the hierarchy of personnel in the newsroom.

The news editor is at its apex. He or she, aided by a deputy, assistant and chief reporter depending on the size of the operation, is the focal point of the newsroom. The newsdesk takes calls from the public, allocates reporters to talk to callers and other story sources, liaises with other departments – especially photography via the picture desk on newspapers – on stories and has a crucial say in which stories are published and the prominence they receive.

Photography is just one of the other departments you will find in a newspaper office. It might be one of your more frequent destinations (to discuss picture arrangements for a story you are working on), but you might also have to visit sport or features. All will be located close to the newsroom, creating a hub of journalistic activity. Around that, and coexisting with it, will be the commercial side of the paper: the advertising and circulation departments – those that make sure your stories are not surrounded by acres of white space (and in effect ensure you are paid, as on average 80 per cent of revenue comes from advertisements) and that ensure customers can read your stories by buying a copy of the paper. Both have to work particularly with a final group of journalists: those in production. They are the ones who have to fit the stories in the paper around advertisements and write headlines and 'bills' (the posters you see on street-corner sellers' stands).

There might be a production editor who takes overall control. But it is as likely that the person in charge will be the chief subeditor. Whichever, he or she is in charge of what goes into the paper. That might mean pruning fifty words from a story so it fits a certain space, rewriting sections, spotting spelling and grammatical errors or cutting anything legally or factually inaccurate. Of course, the production editor or chief sub cannot do all this alone on every story. He or she leads a team of subeditors, each one of whom looks after an individual page or section. They are almost always ex-reporters who have moved into the production side after a stint writing stories.

Obviously, a reporter should write to the length required and avoid making mistakes, but subs are the insurance policy to ensure the most professional product possible. They also put headlines on the stories and marry them with pictures, if relevant. Most important for reporters, subs also dish out bylines – the credit to the writer of a story which says 'By a Reporter'.

In an ideal world a reporter should have as little to do with the subs as possible. Your stories should not need changing, rendering the subs' jobs easier and yours less stressful. Indeed, part of the newsdesk's job is to try to avoid queries by spotting them early and demanding that the reporter clarifies a story or, if it is particularly bad, rewrites it entirely. Clearly, you should try to avoid such demands.

THE NEWSDESK AND THE DIARY

A reporter's relationship with the newsdesk team is vital. Part of making it successful is to know what the news editors expect of you – and what they don't. They will demand you are smart (a visit to court could always be on the news agenda and judges and magistrates insist on standards in their places of work), a good timekeeper (they might be relying on you to do a story the minute you are due in) and equally reliable in other ways (accuracy, for example) as well as self-starting and eager. They do not want to have to tell you how to write each story, who to talk to or what needs to be asked. Nor should they have to insist you work on a certain day or stay late one night. Most of all they will not want you pestering them when they are busy.

The newsroom atmosphere flows like a tide around dead-lines. Every paper or broadcast has a cut-off point after which no more new material can be taken. Obviously, on television or radio it is when the programme ends. Michael Buerk cannot reappear ten minutes after the *Nine o'Clock News* finishes and say, 'And, by the way, here's another story.' Similarly, news-papers have to have a production timetable which deems that the last story for an issue must be written by such a time. It will be slightly more flexible than broadcast deadlines – it can be put back five minutes for a late-breaking story if necessary – but not much. The presses, often with a specific slot booked, have to start rolling to get the paper on the streets. Any delay is printing and selling time lost – and therefore money down the drain.

In every newsroom, activity and tension build up to a climax as a deadline approaches. It could be the main evening dead-line on a national or one of up to half a dozen or more on regional papers with many varying editions or at radio and television stations with regular bulletins. A minute before a deadline, with the news editors calling for copy and rewriting it while fending off calls from the subs, is obviously a bad time to approach the newsdesk to ask for a day off or if they are interested in a story you are working on. It is vital that you know when are the good times, and when the bad, to approach the desk – and, indeed, any of your colleagues who might be on deadline.

It is now time to bring in the other noun, aside from 'newsdesk', which will dominate your journalistic life: the diary. The news editor or one of the deputies will have a daily desk diary. On each day the main news events of which the desk are aware will be entered. For example, a typical week-day's entries might include a court case due for hearing which has been adjourned from another date, a planning committee meeting, the opening of a new hostel by a local VIP and the launch of a new tourist initiative. Other diary entries could range from agricultural shows and collectors' fairs (often a good source of unusual picture stories) to royal visits to the region. Finally, included in the category of 'diary stories' are the regular calls made to the emergency services: each morn-ing and regularly through the day a round of calls will be made to the police, the ambulance and the fire brigade to see if any officers have been sent out on newsworthy incidents. Often there is a rota marked in the diary so that each reporter takes a turn at being responsible for the calls.

In short, the diary contains the stories the newsdesk know are going to happen. For that reason off-diary stories are the ones that the newsdesk cherish. If you can come up with your own stories, and the more often the better, you will be highly regarded. They might include everything from a photo story which came from a card you spotted in a newsagent's window to a child-abuse scandal which a contact in the social services department or police mentioned you might want to look into. Off-diary stories range from tales people did not realise could be news to ones which all too obviously are but which no one would hold a press conference to announce. The common link is that off-diary stories are exclusive – and if there's one thing news editors love, it's an exclusive.

It's worth illustrating the difference between diary and off-diary stories and why news editors are desperate for the latter. Imagine that during a daily call to the police press office you are told the Chief Constable is to hold a press conference. You tell the newsdesk and you attend to hear the area's most senior officer announce he will be retiring. An OK diary story, but one which every other reporter at the news conference has too. But suppose that between being told of the conference and its happening a police contact tells you that the Chief Constable will announce his retirement because he has been caught drink-driving. Not only an off-diary story worth having about the retirement (and before your rivals) but the exclusive angle of the reason for it as well. It would be a guaranteed lead – one no doubt followed up by other reporters up to and including the nationals.

Once more it is worth stressing the timing of your approaches to the newsdesk. The news editor is not going to want to know of your fantastic exclusive five minutes after an edition or bulletin it could have run in has passed. Equally you should not tell them five minutes before deadline. Once you are sure you have the story in place and it is true – *and only then* – tell them about it in a lull in the day so that you can explain exactly what the story is, estimate how much longer it will take to research fully and write, and discuss how to project it. Photographers can be dispatched, graphics commissioned and background reports prepared if necessary. If it's controversial or potentially libellous, the editor can be informed and the pros and cons and standing of the story debated.

One position in which such liaison becomes not just helpful but absolutely essential is if you are sent to work in a district office. Many papers, particularly dailies, have small offices away from the main one. They are in outlying towns or villages as opposed to the city or large town where the title is based. These satellite offices are often one- or two-person operations, and regularly one of those two is a trainee sent for experience of running a diary, dealing direct with the newsdesk every day for every edition, developing contacts and getting under the surface of a particular – and your own – patch. Experience not only of writing stories but also of finding them, sifting the good from the bad and then 'selling' them to the newsdesk.

Be warned, though, that once you have got the newsdesk interested in a story, be it when you are in a district or the head office, you will probably have to deliver it. Like the boy who cried wolf, if you raise too many false alarms, you will eventually be ignored. The *bona fide* scoop you unearth could be underplayed or even discounted because the news editors pay less attention to you than they should, since your alleged off-diary stories have previously turned out to be perhaps nothing more than the work of a fevered imagination and poor reporting skills.

THE WORKING DAY

The routine of your working day will vary depending on your employer: weekly papers generally work from Monday to Friday, with occasional weekend and bank holiday working; daily papers and broadcasters will have shifts covering most of the day and much more weekend and holiday working; and, with the advent of rolling, or twenty-four-hour, news some organisations need round-the-clock staffing 365 days a year.

The beauty of journalism is that vague outline is probably as near as you will get to defining the job in terms of working arrangements. There is no such thing as a 'usual' day, when you know what you will be doing from 9 a.m. to 5 p.m. (if any journalists work such hours: they generally start earlier or later – and work longer than an eight-hour day).

A typical day would start between 8 a.m. and 10 a.m., depending on who you work for (earlier for evening papers and broadcasters with hourly bulletins, later for morning papers with deadlines in the early evening). The news editor might immediately approach you and ask you to make some calls or go out to cover something which has happened over-night or earlier that morning (perhaps even following up a story run by a rival); otherwise you could look at what is in the news that day. It is essential to get into the habit of reading the national papers and catching radio or television news so that you know what is happening and if it has an effect on your local area. Later in the morning, perhaps after first deadlines (which these days are as early as 9 a.m. on evening papers), the newsdesk will give you something to do. It could be a vox pop (asking people their opinion of an issue of the day), a press release which needs developing into a story or covering a court case or a council committee meeting discussing the building of a new housing estate. On a weekly paper a similar range of activities will be spread over the week, culminating in copy day – the week's deadline.

COMPLAINTS AND THE CODE OF CONDUCT

It is better to discover a story is wrong before publication than after. The worst time to wander up to the newsdesk, no matter what time the clock says, is whenever you are doing so to say, 'I've just had a complaint.' Worse still is when, as is more usual, the complainant goes over your head and makes a protest to either the news editor or the editor.

Contrary to popular belief, newspapers take complaints very seriously. Papers cannot afford to alienate the community which they serve – be that the country as a whole or a small village – by printing lies. Their credibility would plummet, readers would fall away and revenue, from sales and advertising, would vanish. True, some national titles have a reputation for inaccuracy, but even they are generally correct. When a celebrity decries the press, it's often because the story is right but they don't want the world to know. For example, the news of Kevin Keegan's resignation as manager of Newcastle United was reported in a national tabloid the day before it was officially confirmed. He tried to discredit the story by suggesting the reporter responsible was unreliable, but Keegan himself was the one who was misleading fans by denying the rumours.

That is not to say, of course, that papers never make mistakes or, indeed, never make things up. But when they do they are usually found out and punished by the regulatory authorities, the libel courts or even disgusted readers who stop buying the paper. And anyone who thinks journalists, editors or proprietors enjoy being dragged through the law courts has never thought about the consequences of having a professional reputation put on the line or the financial implications of massive damages bills.

The most basic deterrent is that no paper or broadcaster likes to have to carry an apology. Not only is it humiliating; it also eats up valuable space and time which could be devoted to stories. Most complaints are resolved long before the need for an apology. Some aren't. Either way, it is the Press Complaints Commission (PCC) which is the regulatory body (at least for print journalists).

Its Code of Practice is the bible of behaviour for reporters, newsdesks, subeditors and editors alike. The eighteen-point document covers accuracy, privacy, harassment and payment for articles as well as intrusion and coverage of crime, including sex cases and discrimination. It defines the public-interest defences which allow breaches of aspects of the code, but, most important for most journalists on a day-to-day basis, it enshrines the right of reply of complainants. Clause 3 of the code reads, 'A fair opportunity for reply to inaccuracies should be given to individuals or organisations when reasonably called for.'

But if that is not enough to satisfy the complainant, the PCC – made up of senior journalists as well as lay members – takes on its more formal role of adjudication. The complainant outlines his or her grievance and asks the PCC to decide if it is justified or not. Every year the PCC receives a couple of thousand complaints. The vast majority either fall outside its remit or are resolved amicably before an adjudication. Of those remaining which require adjudication – only 63 in 1995 – just over half concern accuracy. A similar number are levelled against national newspapers, with the remainder split between regional and local papers, Scottish titles and magazines. But it should be stressed only twenty-eight complaints were upheld of the 2,000 received.

The final recourse for complainants – and a potentially ruinous one for anyone taking it – is to the courts and the libel law. But because of the expense involved and the fact that legal aid is not available, politicians have been concerned about a perceived lack of accountability of the press. The self-regulation of the press via the PCC is not enough, they suggest. But so far 'drinking at the last-chance saloon', to use former Heritage Secretary David Mellor's famous quote about the press's flimsy grip on maintaining the right to self-imposed standards, has not resulted in a hangover. The installation of a majority of lay members to counteract the accusations of pro-industry bias on the PCC seems to have defused calls for privacy legislation or a legal right of reply.

For broadcast journalists the channels of complaint are similar but perhaps less formalised. Executives at a station or channel will be the first to consider a complaint, in discussion with the reporter. If it remains unresolved, there is a variety of different routes for broadcasters. For the BBC, the upper echelons of management will be involved; for ITV, the Independent Television Commission; and for commercial radio, the Radio Authority. Above all of these, as the final judge, is the Broadcasting Standards Commission.

THE NUJ AND EMPLOYMENT ISSUES

There is one body, however, whose ethical code theoretically covers the majority of journalists: the NUJ. Its Code of Conduct differs from other sets of rules in that it is more about the general moral responsibilities of journalists than a list of day-to-day dos and don'ts. The tone is set by the first clause: 'A journalist has a duty to maintain the highest professional and ethical standards.' The subsequent eleven clauses deal with the freedom of the press and censorship, fairness and accuracy, intrusion and dealings with commercial and advertising concerns, as well as discrimination on grounds of gender, colour, race, sexual orientation, disability or marital status. Some cynics might question how closely some of the clauses – particularly the last one mentioned (which is also included in the PCC's code) – are applied by some national tabloid and other newspaper reporters.

There is a good chance, however, that they are not members of the NUJ. The union has 31,000 members – about a third of journalists working in newspapers, magazines, broadcasting and other related areas such as PR. Its main rival, the Institute of Journalists (IoJ), boasts even fewer members: 1,500. Union membership has shrunk dramatically since the 1980s, and the shift towards new technology, which signalled the start of an era of employers paying no official heed to such employees' organisations.

The NUJ and the IoJ still offer legal advice to members and

co-operate in disputes with management, up to and including industrial tribunals. The NUJ also offers other valuable services such as an independent press card, which proves your credentials as a journalist, and sickness and unemployment benefits. Furthermore, it publishes a magazine about journalism, pamphlets about the profession and specific aspects of it and guides to help practitioners in their jobs. It can offer you valuable advice on everything from training colleges to contracts and pay and pensions. Some editors may not like you joining it, or any union, but, as a good journalist, you may have to ask why.

EQUAL OPPORTUNITIES

One area where the union is trying to make headway is in equal opportunities for blacks and other ethnic minorities. There is no firm research on how many members of ethnic minorities are employed in journalism. The NUJ's membership survey put the figure at 1.6 per cent, compared to the 5.5 per cent of the general population. Other research has put the number of staff on national newspapers at between 8 and 12 (of 4,000 or so). The real figure is without question higher (but not much), while broadcasting can boast a higher percentage (but again not much). Regional papers, meanwhile, are suspected of being significantly worse.

The NUJ is about to undertake a comprehensive study of employers asking how many black and ethnic minority people they have on the payroll so that the numbers are known. But, even before the results are published, there is no doubt that a problem exists which needs addressing. In many newsrooms you are most likely to see black faces only when the cleaners or caterers arrive. The cause is not necessarily one of premeditated racism, but of old-fashioned approaches and a type of old-boy network. It is nothing so formal as wearing the right tie to your interview but subconscious attitudes among some who are the gatekeepers to entrance into the profession. They tend to, or at least have tended to, hire in their own image. And very few of them, if any at all, are black. Excluded from 'joining the club' at a training level, blacks are therefore often left in no position to hear of the potential openings to land a first job in the media – perpetuating the final link of what can be a vicious circle.

Ask any black journalist who has broken into the profession and you will almost certainly hear a horror story about appalling treatment. Perhaps not in the first person, but maybe an incident which involved a friend or colleague. Such episodes could range from being mistaken for a secretary or canteen worker to outright and overt racism. In some cases black reporters cannot win: damned if they play down their colour, hoping to push ahead at the same speed as their white colleagues but finding they cannot; damned if they maintain strong links with their own communities, leading to accusations of not wanting to assimilate. It is a situation only likely to improve when newsrooms without black journalists become the exception rather than the rule.

The key to progress is to increase recruitment from the ethnic minorities. In a bid to do so, the NUJ has launched a campaign which includes sponsorship of young black trainees (as have some papers, including the *Guardian*). The George Viner Memorial Fund Trust makes £10,000 a year available to support several applicants. Each has to have been offered a place on a recognised training course and be unable to take it up because of lack of funds from their LEA, an employer or other sponsorship. The amount awarded varies according to the needs of each individual. Some may only have their fees met, others books, travel and accommodation paid for. More details about the fund are available from the NUJ.

Of course, the low numbers of black people in the mainstream press is counteracted by the ethnic press. More than sixty titles exist catering for specific groups or general readerships. Only a tiny fraction are dailies, and the best-known titles, such as the *Voice*, are weeklies. But for aspiring journalists some of these titles can be a less than ideal starting-point: stories abound of poor pay and even worse labour relations. With the NUJ beginning to organise in the sector the situation may improve, but for the time being be wary and check exactly what type of training and prospects are on offer.

The tiny fraction of ethnic-minority respondents in the

NUJ membership survey meant no firm conclusion could be made over pay, although there was some evidence that black journalists are more heavily concentrated at the lower end of the wage scale.

The same is true of women. Whereas one-third of men earned £30,000 or more, only 19 per cent of women did. The disparity increased higher up the pay scale, with 5.3 per cent of men earning more than £50,000 compared to 1.2 per cent of women. Conversely, 26 per cent of women were paid £15,000 or less compared to 18 per cent of men.

Often such discrimination spills over into harassment, according to London College of Printing researchers. Six out of ten women had personal experience or knowledge of such prejudice, while 31 per cent of their male colleagues agreed it existed. Similar figures thought it was more difficult for a capable woman to progress like her male counterparts.

All this is recorded here not to discourage any woman, or any member of an ethnic minority, or any homosexual or lesbian, who would no doubt face similar problems, although with only one in 100 journalists living with a partner of the same sex it is hard to quantify the situation. But this is the situation you must anticipate: this is the world as it is. Of course, you may never have any such problems, but, just in case, forewarned is forearmed.

If determination is the key quality for any journalist, it appears to be even more of a necessity for women or members of minority groups. The situation will probably only improve as female, black and gay journalists break through the 'glass ceiling' into management and – given the first female editor of a regional paper was only appointed this decade and the first female editor of a national broadsheet last year – progress is slow. Perhaps you will be part of the march forward.

PAY AND PLACE

There are fewer controversial factors which influence pay: geography, which branch of the media you work in and, of course, what your job is.

To give an indication of what you might expect to earn, it is illuminating to quote figures which the *Manchester Evening News*, one of the country's leading regional papers, pays its staff. (The figures come from the latest pay discussions, reported in *Press Gazette*.) A trainee can expect to earn between £11,000 and £11,300; qualified journalists between £16,000 and £18,000; experienced journalists between £18,000 and £21,000; and senior journalists between £22,000 and £25,000. The editor chooses into which category staff fall. But it might be fair to assume the four general categories could be something like trainees, newly qualified seniors, subs and specialists and, finally, news editors and other junior executives.

Of course, most papers are smaller than the *Evening News* and therefore the pay is less. The younger you are (and so the shorter your career has been), the less you will be paid. In the NUJ membership survey the group with the largest number being paid under £10,000 – a fifth – was the under twenty-fives. Only 5 per cent earned more than £25,000. In the twenty-five to thirty-four age group, only one in five is earning under £15,000, with almost as many earning more than £30,000. In all the remaining groups until retirement those earning £30,000 or more account for approximately a third.

Pay also varies with location. Four out of ten journalists in Greater London earned £30,000 or more, compared to one in ten in Northern Ireland, Yorkshire and Humberside and the East Midlands. Almost 20 per cent of those in London earned more than £40,000, compared to 0.7 per cent in Northern Ireland and 1.8 per cent in Yorkshire and Humberside. Of course, the cost of living varies from region to region, so bear in mind, when applying for jobs, that being a trainee in London on under £10,000 is far removed from doing the same job on the same salary elsewhere.

Which branch of the media you work in will have an effect on your salary too. The worst-paid sectors – that is, those with the greatest number of people earning under £10,000 – are public relations for charities and independent local radio, both on around 20 per cent. The latter is generally low-paid, with only a quarter earning £25,000 or more. In comparison about half of the BBC regional or local radio staff earn between

£20,000 and £35,000. In newspapers there is a noticeable split between national titles, where one in three earn below £20,000, and provincial ones, where seven out of ten do. In television, a quarter of employees for the national stations earn more than £40,000 (and 10 per cent more than £50,000) compared to 8.6 per cent (and 4.2 per cent) in the regions.

Analysing how much those in each job are paid completes the earnings picture. Two-fifths of reporters earn between £15,000 and £25,000, with one in ten earning more than £40,000 and one in five under £15,000. Just under 16 per cent of subs earn under £15,000, a quarter £15,000–£20,000, more than a third £20,000–£30,000 and one in ten £30,000–£35,000. A third of editors earn under £20,000, another third between £20,000 and £30,000. Almost 6 per cent earn above £50,000. The only job category generally better-paid is broadcasting producer, which has the lowest fraction earning under £20,000 (16.5 per cent) and three in five earning between £25,000 and £40,000.

The morals of all this information appear to be obvious: don't be a young local radio reporter in Northern Ireland or Yorkshire; do try to become a London-based television producer. But, as has been said already, no one comes into journalism to become wealthy. If you want a break in radio and a job comes up in Belfast or Leeds, you will take it. Likewise, if you want to be, say, the health reporter on your home-town paper, the idea of moving to London and into television production is not only ridiculous but utterly irrelevant. And if you want to be rich and work in journalism, your best hope is a lottery ticket or the football pools.

Higher Things

Once you have graduated from being a trainee to a senior reporter two things will probably happen. First, you should get a pay rise, almost certainly your first significant one; second, you might start getting restless. An almost negligible number of journalists remain as a reporter on the same paper for their entire career. One option is to move within the paper, to new positions in other departments or on the newsdesk – and perhaps subsequently management; another, moving on, to break into a new area of journalism by going into PR; a third, to look to joining bigger papers or broadcasters, perhaps in new areas such as features or sport.

As with your entry into journalism, your progression through the profession will not follow any set path. There are general guidelines, of course, which characterise how editors become editors or star foreign correspondents end up over-seas, but no hard-and-fast rules. Again, there is no right or wrong way to secure a dream job or an interim post which might be a useful stepping stone on the way to one.

You need to study the openings which exist carefully and decide which would interest you, which is going to help your career develop in the way you want. When a vacancy appears, consider what is on offer and calculate what you would get from it and whether you would enjoy its new challenges and the changed responsibilities which might come with it. Look before you leap.

STAYING PUT ...

The least risky way to develop your career is to remain at the paper where you trained. You will know the newsroom and how it operates, the people and how they work and the locality and what makes it tick. Your experience and knowledge will not only be valuable to your employer but also make your job easier: no need to learn new names and faces on the newsdesk and their management style, no need to check the spelling of every town and village you write about in a story and no need to develop new contacts. Above all, if it is important to you, no need to relocate, possibly hundreds of miles away from friends and family.

You are unlikely to be offered a new job the day after you qualify. But as a senior you might get bigger stories to cover and extra responsibility while you await the openings. You could be offered – or, better still, suggest – a lengthy off-diary investigation into an issue such as homelessness or drugs; equally you might be asked to run the diary or sit in on the newsdesk at weekends or on other days when the news editors might need assistance. Either way, you will have more input into the paper and the chance to learn about its production and workings.

The most obvious promotion to pursue might be on to the newsdesk. Having proved your journalistic credentials by qualifying, you will be in a position to apply them in the newsroom by spotting stories worth doing from press releases or council agendas, and tweaking copy, or even sending it back to a reporter to be rewritten, where needed. On the newsdesk you will learn about drawing up the newslist and allocating the stories to fill the paper – and the stress which comes from starting each day with both the list and the paper empty.

You will also come into contact with the paper's executives, such as the editor and deputy as well as other heads of department who help define the title's content, look and general ethos. You will have the chance to play a key role in what the paper reports and how those stories are framed. If you have an idea, you can get it put into practice; if you believe a certain topic is worth pursuing, you can deploy reporters to it; if you object to how a particular story was covered, you can voice your thoughts, and they are far more likely to be listened to than similar points raised when you were a junior reporter.

Given the power, it is unsurprising that some news editors can verge on megalomania. But if they were not self-confident, they would be all too like George, the mild-mannered but ineffective news editor in *Drop the Dead Donkey*. And there is a downside for even the most cocksure newsdesk executives: they are anonymous beyond the paper. Stories do not carry their name even if they rewrite half of them, and the awards handed out to reporters for excellence are never shared with the newsdesks which encouraged it and, in some cases, magnified it.

An even more discreet, but no less vital, job is that of the subeditor. You may decide after your training that you want to move from the gathering of news to the processing of it. If you trained on a small paper, you might have had some subbing experience as part of the all-hands-to-the-pump approach. Alternatively, you might have done some subbing at college or just want to move away from the frontline of reporting – including coming face to face with bereaved relatives of accident victims or having to stand in the rain conducting a vox pop – to an entirely office-based existence. Perhaps you have an eye for design or skill at editing, rather than writing, which would be best deployed on the subs' table.

That phrase, and the term 'backbench' – meaning the small group of senior journalists, such as the editor and chief sub, who oversee all the news pages – are anachronisms based on furniture which has long gone. Today the subs' table and the backbench are likely to look the same as the rest of the newsroom: desks with PC terminals on them. But both play the same role they always have.

In addition to the subs' main duties – checking copy for spelling, contextual and legal errors and fitting text into designated spaces – they also turn stories which, when written, look much like the text of this book into columns, with bylines and rules between them. They also key in instructions on the size of the typeface to be used and any variations in it as the story runs, provide captions to accompany pictures and 'crop' (that is, edit to size) the pictures themselves.

But perhaps the most skilful part of the subs' job is distilling a story of anything up to 1,500 words or more into a headline of probably under ten, often under five. The type of headline varies from paper to paper, from the puns and fun of the *Sun* to the more considered and drier intonations of the broadsheets. To give an example, when Paymaster General David 'Two Brains' Willetts resigned over his duplicitous role in the cash-for-questions scandal at Parliament the *Sun*'s headline was 'Two Brains, Two Faces, but No Job', while the *Guardian*'s was 'Willetts pays the price'. Just like reporters, subs have to work to the style of their paper.

Subbing is not for everyone, but one aspect to be considered before dismissing it out of hand is that it is rare to become an editor without subbing experience. An editor oversees the manufacture of the entire newspaper, so if he or she is lacking in production skills, there is a large gap in their knowledge – and one which is difficult to overcome. Editors do not need to have taken on every role in their career – for example, if they lack sports knowledge, it is not too important because they have specialists with great expertise to report on that topic – but understanding the workings of the paper's creation is one skill which cannot be ignored. It would be akin to a football manager being incapable of kicking a ball himself.

... AND RISING IN THE HIERARCHY: THE EDITOR

The first senior journalist you ever talk to is likely to be an editor, during an interview for a job. Remember they once sat in your place, nervous as they met someone who could give them their first break into journalism. It may have been fifty years ago or five, but you can be sure they know how you are feeling. They also know what made them the successful journalist they are and will be looking for similar qualities in you.

Many editors have not set out to become one. They might

have entered journalism for the same reasons as you want to – a burning desire to know what's going on and report on it – but realised they did not want to spend their entire career reporting. They may have found, perversely, that their talents for spotting stories and covering them comprehensively actually took them away from being a reporter and into management. Or they may have veered off into subbing and discovered they had the flair for design which characterises many good editors.

The variety of routes to the summit means there is a variety of styles of editorship. Some editors are gung-ho and model themselves on the former editor of the *Sun*, Kelvin McKenzie; others see themselves as the quality journalists' journalist and nurture gifted reporters and columnists while taking a back seat themselves. Some remain star subs who come up with snappy headlines and natty new designs; others continue as writers, contributing leaders, columns, interviews, reviews and even news. Sadly, some also see their job as no more than managing decline and meeting owners' demands for greater and greater tightening of the editorial budget.

Whatever their style, they have certain duties in common, more specific than the general overseeing of the paper. First and foremost, as far as the young reporter is concerned, they hire, and fire, staff and have a large say in promotions and transfers from one department to another. They host the news conference and decide which stories will get the most prominence. They are assumed in law to have seen the entire content of the paper, so that if a serious legal problem arises, it is they who are ultimately responsible. Editors, not reporters, subs or even proprietors, can be jailed in such cases. For example, the publishers and editors of the *Daily Record* and Scottish *Sun* were fined – £5,000 and £250 respectively – in May 1996 for printing illegal stories about a sex offender; in contrast, the reporters who wrote them saw the cases against them dismissed after judges took the view that the stories were submitted for legal scrutiny and it was not the reporters' fault that the material had been published.

Editors also strike the tone for the paper and become its public face. When a reporter comes across a big story it is the editor who decides whether to run it or not. They will encourage their staff to concentrate on certain topics or subjects – for example, 'sleaze' or the monarchy – and take responsibility for what is unearthed, if it is subsequently reported. For that reason it is the editor who appears on television when a certain paper produces a great scoop or is at the centre of a controversy. And it is he or she who may later have to reprise the role before the PCC or a libel jury.

The editor also sets down a paper's stance on issues it reports, sometimes after consulting with colleagues. On a local paper it might mean whether the title supports plans for a town-centre redevelopment or a new bypass; nationally it is more likely to be on matters such as European integration (which could have originally led to the funding for the town-centre plans) or policy issues. However, editors do not edit in a vacuum. An evening-paper editor is not going to oppose a redevelopment or new road if it is clear most of the readers are staunchly behind it. Equally the editor of conservative papers such as the *Daily Telegraph* or *Mail* is not going to welcome a single European currency or the abandonment of road building in favour of generous state-funded public transport.

Editors cannot do entirely as they please. Papers – and in this case it is papers (and national ones far more than local) rather than radio or television – have a political stance, either from tradition or the proprietor, or both. Those views can be fluid: for example, the traditional, conservative *Financial Times* supporting Labour in the 1992 election and arch-Tory Rupert Murdoch's wooing of the party's subsequent leader, Tony Blair. One of Murdoch's papers, *Today*, even went so far from his usual agenda as to declare itself Green. But, in general, tradition counts for more. When Labour supporter Lord Hollick took over the historically Conservative *Express* titles he promised he would not alter their politics.

Such tradition, and proprietorial interference when it occurs, can only make an editor's job more difficult. While being wary of the law and the day-to-day difficulties of production on one hand, they have to be wary of upsetting loyal readers or the ultimate bosses on the other. The former might object to a story being reported on grounds of taste or content;

the latter, for political or financial reasons. On a local paper in a rural area an editor might run into trouble for trying a more modern design or giving some sympathy to anti-hunt protesters. On a national the use of bad language in a headline of a conservative title (as when the *Sunday Express* used the word 'shits') or the perceived 'tabloidisation' of a serious broadsheet might create similar problems.

As regards politics itself, there is some debate over how influential the views handed down by any paper, via the editor and the proprietor, are. Titles such as the *Sun*, in particular, are clearly partisan, often obviously so. The *Sun* itself claimed that its own front page on the day of the 1992 election – which asked whoever was last to leave the country after a Labour victory to turn off the lights – won the election for the Tories. It later watered down its claims and they have been subjected to much analysis since.

But the one fact worth noting, as far as young journalists entering the profession are concerned, is the impact such slanted reporting can have on them. Staff working on right-wing titles will be asked to do pieces on alleged abuses of the welfare state and immigration rules or 'knocking' pieces on Labour's tax or defence plans. That may all sit uncomfortably with any left-of-centre views they might hold. They still have to write them. But do not think they all believe what they write. Almost six out of ten journalists are Labour supporters and only 6 per cent Tories, according to London College of Printing research. It is a question, as was said in the introduction, of being able to report the stories no matter what your personal views.

MOVING ON

Regardless of any affection you may have for your first paper, even if you have moved to a new job in subs or another department, a better one within the newsroom or even editing, you will almost certainly move on at some stage, though some journalists will stay on the same title, or ones closely related by ownership and geography, for all their careers. Some editors are increasingly calling for such loyalty rather than the attitude of the 'have notebook, will travel' university graduates who are always looking for bigger and better opportunities, passing through small town or big city on the way to national papers and magazines. But the reality is that small papers can rarely afford to pay for such loyalty.

Editors are frequently unable to meet the quite reasonable demands of often highly educated and highly trained staff who, by their mid-twenties expect to be on a salary of more than around £13,000. Their friends who went into accountancy or law might be earning twice as much. Even a reporter who starts on a small daily paper and, after qualifying as a senior reporter, moves on to the newsdesk and even becomes news editor would probably be earning less than the national average wage for white-collar workers (which is £21,000). In the words of the NUJ: 'If you are bright and intelligent enough to have got in journalism and qualified, you will probably realise you cannot afford to stay put.'

Furthermore, any journalist with ambitions to develop their reporting skills rather than moving into subbing or on to the newsdesk will have to move. Such ambitions are often fulfilled by becoming a 'specialist' covering, for example, crime, education, health or social services. But small papers, both weekly and daily, cannot afford to have specialists. It is only the bigger city dailies and the nationals which have such correspondents. They might be your next destination.

SPECIALISMS

A specialist's job is to become an expert in a given field, while retaining the attributes of a general reporter. They are expected to bring general news judgement to their particular area, spotting stories in the 'trade' press devoted to their subject and developing contacts with figures in the field. As well as finding the stories and reporting, an important part of a specialist's job is to set them in context or explain what the developments being reported mean. And that in-depth knowledge also means newsdesks rely on specialists to monitor stories run by rivals or suggested by freelances to decide which are worth following up. Specialists will also be expected to contribute to any feature pages set aside, often weekly, for detailed coverage of their subject.

In recent years a whole series of new specialisms, such as environment, media, sports news and even, on the down-market tabloids, the National Lottery, have sprung up. Indeed, the latter job itself created a story when Lenny Lottery, a reporter who changed his name by deed poll, defected from the *Sun* to the *Mirror*. His very existence illustrates how a specialist post often comes to be: a new topic provokes much interest, prompting the need for an in-house expert rather than a succession of general reporters to handle the stories arising from it, and one of those general reporters is briefed to cover the beat. Changing their name, as Lenny did, is not compulsory.

Among the types of story which have caused the creation of such new specialists are global warming (environment) and digital television (media). Perhaps the biggest growth area, however, is showbusiness. The tabloids have long had show-biz editors. Now, though, they head teams of reporters. The broadsheets have not gone so far as to appoint such showbiz specialists themselves, but they are covering the same stories. Think of Hugh Grant's embarrassing incident in Los Angeles in 1995 or the on-off split of Oasis in 1996: both were covered as thoroughly and prominently in the 'upmarket' broadsheets as in the 'downmarket' tabloids.

In general it is the broadsheets, nationally, and the big-city papers, locally, which have the larger teams of specialists. On the nationals they will probably outnumber the general reporters and include every subject from the arts to sport via religious affairs and politics; in the provinces they are more likely to be in the minority, with perhaps only councils, education, health and crime covered. But specialists and the detailed reporting they produce are vital to both types of paper. They provide the detail and depth of coverage which are important selling points.

In some ways specialists are therefore the élite of the newsroom, tackling the most important areas – those thought to be of most concern to readers. But even so the regional press in general has seen a decline in specialists and the rise of all-rounders, no doubt partly because of the perceived luxury and cost of having reporters who might not write more than one story a day. Meanwhile, the nationals have cut back on certain specialisms considered less important now than in the past. For example, labour, once a key area (often with a team of reporters devoted to it), is now often merged with another subject, if it exists at all.

So how do you become a specialist? The first stumbling block is that on the rare occasions when any such jobs are advertised, either in the *Guardian* or *Press Gazette* or by word of mouth, the applicants are expected to have knowledge and experience of the relevant area. It stands to reason: an education reporter must know about the structure of the school, college and university system and issues affecting it; he or she cannot spend six months learning about them before filing a début specialist story – the newsdesk will want informed, and ideally exclusive, coverage from day one. But it is a Catch-22 situation: you cannot become a specialist without experience, but you cannot get experience without being a specialist. What you have to do is make yourself experienced.

If there is a certain area which interests you and which you know about, offer the newsdesk stories about it, develop contacts relating to it and monitor other media for possible developments you can cover. No newsdesk is going to discourage such enthusiasm. If there is an existing correspondent in the field you are interested in, however, do not go behind their back to the newsdesk. Offer them the stories instead and tell them you are available to do any stories they have not got time to do or cover for them when they are away. If the post becomes vacant, you will have a good chance of stepping straight into it; if it does not, you at least have the cuttings and experience other editors seek; and if the specialism has not previously existed, perhaps you can convince the newsdesk or the editor of the need to create it.

As well as becoming a specialist on a local or regional paper and sticking with the topic as your career develops, perhaps to the nationals, there is a second, parallel route: the trade or other specialist press, which is almost exclusively based in London. *Press Gazette* belongs in this category: it covers a particular industry or topic and that alone. Other examples are *Broadcast* (television), *The Times Education Supplement* (schools) or the *British Medical Journal* (health). A job on such a title could lead to an appointment as a national newspaper's specialist reporter. Throughout national newsrooms there are reporters, and executives, who have worked on at least one of the titles mentioned above. They have the specialist knowledge, but also the reporting skills. Many of them started on local papers in the first place and then moved into the trade press.

Some say that specialising means you are forgoing the chance of editorship. This might have once been the case, with production skills being more valued in prospective executive material than in-depth knowledge of, for example, NHS reforms. No longer, judging by the nationals. The deputy editor of the *Guardian* is the paper's ex-media correspondent (and was formerly with *Broadcast*) and the *Independent*'s editor was a political specialist. Max Hastings, until 1996 one of the longest-serving editors after ten years at the helm of the *Daily Telegraph*, was a defence correspondent, while the youngest national editor, Piers Morgan of the *Mirror*, was a showbiz specialist less than five years ago. Today cross-media recruitment, from non-traditional routes such as the trade press and even consumer glossy magazines, is common: the ultimate proof was when Rosie Boycott was appointed the first woman editor of a national broadsheet (the *Independent on Sunday*) after being editor of the men's monthly *Esquire*. It is becoming more and more the case that to reach the top it's less what you've done than the way that you've done it that is important.

NEWS AGENCIES AND FREELANCING

Another way to move away from local papers and even get stories in the nationals is by freelancing. That could mean setting up as a one-man or -woman band, using your news sense, contacts and determination to discover stories yourself and sell them to papers. Or it could mean joining a freelance agency, where you would be most likely to be on the staff. The agency would sell your stories.

Both can offer new opportunities and the chance to pursue stories you want. But neither is ideal for many journalists: freelancing individually can be a precarious occupation, with success – and therefore income – subject to the whims of newsdesks and what else is happening on any given day; agencies can mean working exceptionally hard with no rewards in print – national staffers in London use submitted copy as the basis of a story with their byline on it – and often poor pay.

The market for both freelances and agencies comes from one simple fact: no newspaper, however big its circulation or the size of its staff, can hope to cover every story. There are simply too many, often off-diary and therefore impossible for a newsdesk to prepare for. Additionally, in the case of nationals, the tales are often in places far away from the limited number of reporters they have in the provinces. They rely on freelances to inform them of what is going on in vast areas of the country. That might mean a stringer – a reporter who submits stories on spec to a newsdesk or is paid a retainer to file to a particular title first – or agencies, which basically operate as outposts of the national press.

Both are paid on the basis of how much of a story is used. If none is, they are generally not paid, which leads to uncertain finances for the freelances, but has obvious advantages for the papers. A staffer covering a remote, non-newsy patch may have a run of several days without a story and will still have to be paid. A freelance's quiet days cost the paper nothing.

For an individual wanting to freelance in news journalism outside London the best advice is almost certainly: don't. Quite simply, it is highly unlikely you will make enough money to survive, let alone justify the number of hours you will have to put in. If you doubt it, pick an area – perhaps your own home town – and count the number of stories in or around it that are printed in the nationals. If there are any, multiply the numbers of words in them by 20p and you will get a rough estimate of what you might be paid for that story. Multiply that by how many stories make the paper each week to guesstimate income and then by fifty-two for an annual total. Take away overheads – such as the cost of a computer (up to

£2,000), office rent, bills (telephone, electricity and station-ery), mobile phone costs and tax – before considering any of the money as wages. And don't forget that you would have to have beaten whoever really provided the stories to the papers before making a penny.

Of course, you could try to supply local or regional papers and broadcast stations with tip-offs and to write for national magazines, such as the large number of women's titles or football, music or other publications which always need stringers. The problem is the former are likely to have much of the area amply covered and, even so, pay poorly, while the latter might want pieces only infrequently. And you will still be competing with established freelances who usually have good contacts, both for finding stories and placing them, perhaps after many years of working in the area and/or being a staffer on one of the publications which needs freelance copy. If you want to try your hand at freelancing, by all means give it a go – but before you start you will have to be very realistic about your potential markets and income.

Working for an agency is a more financially secure way of tackling the type of stories which appear in the national papers and news-based magazines. Every town has one agency or more. They compete mainly against each other, but also against the local media on middling stories and the nationals – to beat them to the story and hence sell it to them – on bigger ones. Some comprise only one or two people, perhaps a reporter and a photographer; others, such as Birmingham-based Newsteam, which also operates in both the north-west and the north-east of England, have almost as many staff as some of the smaller titles they serve. Some have a clear run on stories, following up ones from local papers as well as develop-ing their own, while others have fierce competition. At present in the north-east there are four competing agencies, not to mention several individual freelances.

The bread and butter for agencies are diary stories: court, emergency calls and the big set-piece visits. They are generally looking for human-interest stories – ones about people and what they have done or has been done to them – as these are the tales the tabloids want. And it is the tabloids that provide agencies' main market – because they pay better and have a greater demand for stories, particularly exclusives. When a page lead in a broadsheet might make you only £100 while a shorter story in a tabloid could make five times as much or more, it does not need an accountant to work out where the more lucrative business is.

Agencies might also take on commissions from London-based newsdesks, or ones from overseas if the story is big enough, to cover a local angle. That might mean anything from a vox pop or a court case to confronting a big celebrity who has just been, or is just about to be, exposed as being guilty of some sort of wrongdoing. Commissions might also include filing reports and, more likely, pictures from football matches or other sporting fixtures.

The television series *Harry*, starring Michael Elphick as the head of a small northern agency, made clear one of the pitfalls of being a freelance: if you're not careful, you can have many contacts and no friends, while your working life sometimes spills over into your real life. Some freelances are unpopular with other journalists working in the same area. There is nothing more irritating for a local reporter who unearths a great story for his or her paper than to see a freelance pick it up and sell it on. Or for the local journalist who goes out to try to interview someone only to find a freelance has got there first, with a chequebook backed by a national title, and has bought up the subject of the story. Freelances themselves would argue if staffers are so upset by the competition, they should try surviving in such a cut-throat market. And they have a point: if you tried to sell a story you wrote for your paper to a national, and got caught, you could be sacked. It's probably wiser to develop a discreet relationship with freelances and perhaps offer them your stories – on the condition of only selling it on after publication in your paper and for a small tip-off fee – than ignore them.

PUBLIC RELATIONS AND OTHER POSSIBLE CAREERS

Another group with whom you will have to develop a relationship are press officers or public relations officers, collectively known as PRs. Almost every story written nowadays has some PR involvement, ranging from the story itself coming from a press release to a press officer providing an official response or information. In each case the role of the PR is vital: in the first, finding, even perhaps 'creating', the story; in the latter two, making an official statement (which might have taken days if a chief executive, chairman or chief constable had to be contacted personally).

For journalists PR has another attraction: a possible career. Many organisations, both in the private and the public sector, are keen to recruit journalists into their press offices. In the sense that such a career choice would mean moving from chasing the news and more into managing it, it can be argued PRs are poachers-turned-gamekeepers. But in almost every way PRs remain journalists; all that has changed is their employer. PRs still have to find an angle on a story and write it up – except it is then called a press release; many still have to find human-interest stories and enliven dull financial reports, but instead of doing so for the local paper, they will be doing it for an even more narrowly based publication: the in-house newspaper. Yet they still have to know the right questions to ask, even if only so they can brief their superiors on what to expect from the press.

The vast majority of journalists would say – and not just because of self-interest – that the best PRs are those who have come from a journalistic background. They know what news-desks expect and they appreciate deadlines. They don't ask, as do some PRs who have never been journalists, 'I don't see what that's got to do with the story,' or 'Why do you want to know that?' However, there is a growing trend for PRs to have no journalistic background; some may have even done the dreaded media studies course. The result can be a breakdown in communications.

There's nothing more annoying for a journalist than a jobsworth PR who thinks their task is not to help the press but to tell them as little as possible – and, ideally, nothing. At the same time there's nothing more galling for a PR than spending hours preparing a press release, and subsequently explaining a story, only to read a report which is inaccurate or, perhaps worse still, not see a report at all. But the antipathy which sometimes bubbles to the surface of the press–PR relationship does little to hide the amount the two need each other.

If reporters had to call senior management every time they wanted to check a fact or get a quick quote, their job would take two or three times as long; and if newsdesks had to unearth every single story to which they assigned reporters rather than occasionally opening the post and pulling out a decent press release, their jobs would be even more tricky than they already are. Meanwhile if every company, voluntary group or council had to deal with the press on an ad hoc basis rather than having a designated PR, some people would never get a jot of other work done. Chief executives and chief constables, executives and beat bobbies are not employed to spend all their time dealing with the press. But these people and their PRs also need the press to convey an image or theme to the public or to tell the world what is going on in their company or organisation. Clearly, if PR didn't exist, someone would have to invent it.

At the lowest levels PR and journalism can overlap in the same person. A reporter on a local paper might also be press liaison officer for a scout troop, a football team or a mothers' group. The voluntary position might only involve publicising dates of meetings or results via the local paper, but it is still, in its humble way, PR. And if a bigger event occurred – say, a royal visit to a group's HQ or a good run in the FA Cup – the PR might find him- or herself tied up in the type of work full-time PRs might have to worry about: accreditation for reporters, communications facilities and a timetable. Not to mention refreshments.

Once PR becomes your career, however, there is a change. No matter how much is made of the general similarities between journalists in the media and those in PR, there is one vital, basic difference when the two come into contact: a journalist's job is about asking questions to uncover the truth; a PR's is to answer them – and sometimes in such a way as to 'spin' the truth. In reality such conflicts of interest are rare. Only relationships between certain groups – for example, environment reporters and big-business PRs or crime reporters and police press officers – have the potential to descend into acrimony because of a clash of objectives. It should be stressed that most PRs and journalists coexist quite happily.

And that is partly enforced: because of the ubiquity of PR, journalists have to accept they can't live without it, however much they would like to. PRs work in business, sport, politics and government (under the title of 'information officers'). If you want an interview with a leading figure in any of these worlds, you will have to go via their PR. To use a police example again, if you want to know anything from the chief constable's view on drugs to how many officers are in the drugs squad or how many people were arrested for drugs offences in a given year, your starting-point is most likely to be a PR.

Sometimes they may not want to help you. They might claim a certain topic is not one they want to discuss – and then they offer an alternative. This is the start of the type of PR known as 'spin doctoring'. Generally, although not exclusively, its practitioners are PRs whose role is less to liaise with journalists on their stories than to influence a story or feed an entire line to either a single reporter or a pack of them, to say, 'You don't want to write about that. This is the story.' It is the ultimate pro-active PR, rather than passive response to reporters' queries.

This is PR in both its crudest and its most subtle forms: heavily influencing what is reported, but doing so in the most behind-the-scenes way. The practitioners of such 'black arts', as one Labour frontbencher called them, end up being as well known – and reviled by some – as those they serve: Mrs Thatcher's spokesman, Sir Bernard Ingham, once of the *Guardian*, and Alastair Campbell, former political editor of the *Daily Mirror* and Sir Bernard's equivalent in the court of Tony Blair, are perhaps the best examples.

Going into PR as a career move has its advantages. If you are disillusioned with any aspect of life on a paper or in broadcasting, PR probably offers an escape. It is, as a rule, better paid, the hours are generally not as arduous (although you can be on call whenever journalists are) and the potential for moving in a new direction may prove to be a clincher.

From PR you can move into general corporate life and progress through the managerial side of a business or organisation, if you decide that is what interests you more.

But if you are tempted into PR beware of the one main disadvantage: it can be very difficult to switch back to journalism. Some employers in the media would see the letters PR on your CV and wonder about your commitment: you were prepared to give up what they might see as 'real journalism' once – would you do so again?

It is not impossible, however, to return to journalism if you leave for a while, whatever the reason. After all, there are no real rules about getting in, so why should there be about getting out and back in again? But it can be difficult, perhaps partly because of the personal circumstances you might find yourself in: if you get accustomed to better pay and shorter hours, you might rather not return to reporting.

Moving into PR is a legitimate career route, and one taken by many journalists, but, perhaps more than with any other choice in your career, think long and hard about it. It is likely to be the decision that is harder than any others to reverse. Equally, it is probably best not to go into PR, as your first job in the media, thinking you will eventually move into journalism. Again, it is not impossible, just very, very unlikely. Editors want to see journalists who have a burning ambition to be journalists, not those who just want a job in the media and quite fancy giving reporting a go.

OTHER OPTIONS

Of course, PR is not the only alternative route opened up by starting your career in journalism. If you have shown you can write, there will be other opportunities to work as a writer: perhaps as a script or screen writer, an author or a novelist. To give two examples, one well known, the other less so: playwright Tom Stoppard, a reporter on local papers in Bristol throughout the 1950s, once said, 'I got a bigger thrill from seeing my first by-line . . . than from having my first play on at the National [Theatre]'; more than forty years later a part-time *Bradford Telegraph and Argus* sub called Martyn Bedford also saw success with creative writing when the rights to his first novel were bought for £100,000.

You might not scale such heights, but if you can write, you can write. Just like journalists, authors and other writers don't need a badge that proves they can do their job. They just do it. And once you have proved you can string a sentence together, there are many options open to you. You might make continued use of your writing skills, whether writing press releases, copy for advertisements or scripts for news programmes and even drama. Your strength with words might be developed in the most glamorous ways – for example, Neil Tennant, singer and lyricist with the Pet Shop Boys, is an ex-reporter (on *Smash Hits*) – or the more mundane.

If you have a specialism, your options are increased further. There is a regular stream of, for example, financial journalists getting jobs in the City or media pundits being signed up as analysts with advertising firms. One journalist who has followed such a path, and whom you will see regularly, is David Davies, the Football Association's public figurehead, who for many years was a regional news and national sports presenter with the BBC.

In Parliament too there have been many who once sat in the Press Gallery and then moved to the Government or Opposition benches. Ex-Tory minister Norman Fowler, a former Home Affairs Correspondent with *The Times*, and Labour's Austin Mitchell, a television journalist who worked for Granada and the BBC before his election and for Sky subsequently, are perhaps two of the best-known.

But if such grand careers do not appeal, a grounding in news journalism also provides the opportunity to branch out in more low-key or altruistic areas. For example, with the advent of desk-top publishing, there are many ex-reporters who have formed their own small printing companies. Others have transferred campaigning skills from their journalistic careers and applied them to other areas. Perhaps the best example of such a lobbyist is Marjorie Wallace, an ex-*Sunday Times* journalist, now chief executive of the mental-health charity Sane.

Journalism itself can be a fantastic career. But perhaps one of its greatest advantages is that you can conceivably do it for a couple of years and then see a whole new field of opportunities open up before you. If, for any reason, you fall out of love with the profession, there are dozens of related but alternative careers awaiting you. You could change your job significantly without having to change your profession completely.

Paul Myers, aged thirty-five, is a subeditor on the *Guardian* and one of the small number of black journalists. A graduate in French and German, he completed an NCTJ block-release course after joining a weekly paper in south London. He then worked as a reporter on an evening paper and shifted for national papers and broadcasters. He switched to subbing when he went to work in Paris.

I was working for Agence France-Presse in Paris, translating articles and subbing, but still reporting, in effect, because I would be rewriting if there were not direct translations.

One of the things that made me switch to subbing full-time when I got back from France was that there was no point me coming back and doing the same thing as before I left. I wanted to enrich my skills base and get more experience.

What I was doing over there was living off my reporter's instincts; what I got back here was training in how to write headlines and how to cut copy down.

The differences with subbing are that you have to be a bit more precise about spelling and grammar and look at things with a fresh eye, so where things don't follow through, you rearrange them. Reporters can get too close to stories.

From the newsdesk, stories are sent to the chief sub, who plans the pages and works out how much space each one will get. They are then sent on to subs like me, who edit the text if necessary and write the headline, before going to the revise sub, who checks what's been done and then sends them through to go into the paper.

Becoming a sub does not have to mean the end of your writing career. It is possible still to write – and in many ways the reason I'm doing it is to become a better writer in the long term as well as getting a new skill.

As to which is more enjoyable, reporting or subbing, they are both exciting. Asking questions, that's what everyone imagines journalism to be – getting your foot in the door and so on. But it can be just as satisfying writing a good headline as having your name on the front-page splash.

I think because of my colour I've always made sure of getting proper qualifications and experience, so that I couldn't be fobbed off at job interviews by somebody saying, 'You need to go and do this.' When I went from the weekly to the *Nottingham Evening Post* a friend said I shouldn't bother and should just try to get some shifts straight away – but he knew why I was doing it and why it was necessary.

Employers now often want more people from the ethnic minorities and I think it will be easier for the next generation –just as it was easier for my generation than the one before.

But there is still an attitude sometimes that you should be grateful for what you've got and shut up and accept it. It's almost a 'massa' mentality and that's where the problems can start at work.

The hopes and aspirations and dreams of members of the black community are as diverse as those of the white community. It's important if you are black that you don't just get in and then sit back. We've got to show people we want more.

Fleet Street and the Nationals

There is no getting away from the fact that when many people talk about 'what's in the papers' or ask, 'Did you see the story about so-and-so?' they are talking about the national press. The 1,500 local and regional papers sell millions of copies, but the twenty national daily titles sell about 13 million copies each day. The *Sun* alone sells more than 4 million daily – almost as much as the entire regional daily press combined. On Sundays, the nationals sell another 15 million copies – an even more pronounced lead over the sprinkling of regional Sunday titles, which sell only about 2.3 million (with the vast majority of that coming from two quasi-national Scottish titles, the *Sunday Post* and the *Sunday Mail*).

When curbs are threatened to counter the alleged excesses of reporters and their editors, the catalyst for the discussions is something the nationals have done, even though such moves would affect every paper, big or small. And the best stories – intrusive or in the public interest, the secrets of Pamela Anderson's boudoir or Tony Blair's Cabinet table – are generally broken by the nationals. The big-name interviews, often by equally big-name interviewers, appear in their pages, as does the most comprehensive arts and sports coverage.

It is therefore not surprising that many – but by no means even a majority of – journalists aspire to work on what is known as Fleet Street. They see the chance to report or sub the biggest stories, for bigger audiences, and to be sent all over the country (and globe), all while being part of the community at the pinnacle of the press in this country.

There are many reasons to avoid working for the nationals:

the hours can be even longer than in the regions, with pay sometimes still not matching the effort put in; the stress, caused by fierce competition and even fiercer newsdesks, can be overwhelming; and London – perceived by some as expensive, dirty and unfriendly (although it has recently well-documented cultural and social advantages) – is still where you will almost certainly have to move to if you want to pursue a career on the nationals. It is by no means everyone's definition of an ideal city to call home. You could also find yourself competing for jobs, and possibly stories too, against your friends. On some papers, you will be expected to forfeit your entire life outside work if you want to break in and make a name for yourself. And it can take years of struggling as a freelance, being at the beck and call of newsdesks and enduring a certain amount of financial uncertainty, before you might get that break and land a staff job.

If – and it is a big if – you want to try your luck on the nationals, you have to accept all of the above and be prepared to endure it. Even then, and despite your best efforts, your chance may never come. But even those whose luck has eluded them will probably agree that it is better to have tried and failed than never to have tried at all.

FLEET STREET

It is the most famous location in the British press, synonymous with national newspapers. But it is also now entirely stripped of them. Once, walking its length would have meant mingling with scores of journalists from the newspaper offices lining it, as well as with the printers and other staff involved in the production of the most famous titles in the land. Every one was based on or just off Fleet Street. Now the eagle-eyed might spot the former HQs of the *Daily Mail* or the Press Association, the national agency. But no one would guess the street's former role as the heart of the newspaper business.

There has been a bypass operation. The various titles are now scattered all over London. The nearest equivalent to Fleet Street, in terms of concentration of newspaper offices, is probably Canary Wharf in Docklands, east London, home to both the *Daily* and the *Sunday Telegraph* and all the Mirror Group titles (the *Mirror*s, the *Independent*s and the *People*). News International (*The Times*, the *Sunday Times*, the *Sun* and the *News of the World*) are based near by in Wapping, while the Mail titles – including London's *Evening Standard* – the *Express* and the Scott Trust (the *Guardian* and the *Observer*) are respectively in Kensington, Blackfriars and Farringdon.

The geographical changes are of little importance themselves, but crucial in what they illustrate and result from: the computerisation of the newspaper industry. An entrepreneur named Eddie Shah, with a background in local newspapers, started the revolution when he launched the now deceased *Today* in 1985. But it was when Rupert Murdoch took his titles to Wapping, in a move designed, successfully, to break the power of the printers over the production process, that change began apace. The News International move allowed newspapers to exploit new technology without the restraint of what were seen as old labour practices. A bitter and sometimes violent dispute, which eventually ended in defeat for the printing unions, followed. The newspaper industry was never the same again.

That became very obvious with an off-shoot of the *Today* and News International developments: the *Independent*. It was devised by journalists who realised new technology could mean an opportunity for launching a new broadsheet – Britain's first for well over a century. And it was also largely staffed by journalists who were disillusioned by Murdoch and the Wapping dispute. The *Independent* could not have been created without both the new technology and the old know-how.

The technology also led to an explosion in supplements, from style, arts and review sections in the Sunday papers to pull-outs in the dailies, such as the separate sports sections which almost every title now has at least once a week. Again, it meant new openings for journalists, not general reporters perhaps, but anyone with such a basic grounding could, and still can, exploit the increased demand. Someone who could spot the type of story these new supplements demanded and turn them out, was – and is – away. Alan Rusbridger, now editor of the *Guardian*, but formerly the features editor who introduced the paper's tabloid section, wrote in 1988: 'My sense is that there is much more scope for the talented and hard-working freelance in London [than ten years earlier] . . . Anyone with talent and determination will eventually make it.'

But he berated the quality of the copy he received from freelances who were 'graduates in their mid-twenties who have drifted into journalism . . . with the hazy notion of writing about "the arts" or "doing interviews" '. What they lacked, he said, was a spell on a local paper, learning about intros and pay-off lines, structure and style. The conclusion, from a journalist who started his career as a news reporter on the *Cambridge Evening News*, was this: 'At the risk of sounding old-fogeyish, a spell of writing about washeteria break-ins would do some of them no harm at all.'

STAFF AND SHIFTING

If you have remained a reporter and followed the usual route, you will perhaps have worked on two or three ever larger local papers, reporting on bigger and better stories, honing your story-getting and story-telling skills. You could progress on to the newsdesk or into subbing or features. Alternatively, you could have looked towards broadcasting or PR. But if you want to stay as a print reporter, and continue upwards, your next step might be the nationals. The same applies to subs and sports reporters ready to move on from the provinces.

You will know how the nationals vary as products from the *Sport* and the *Morning Star* on the fringes to the *Sun* and the *Guardian* in the mainstream. What unites them is that, no matter how much you want to work for them, you will almost certainly not get a staff job immediately. Because so many people want to work on nationals – and their editors have to ensure those who do are of sufficient calibre – they can afford to be miserly in handing out jobs. Once, under the more formal system of the 1950s and 1960s, journalists who had done three years or more on the regionals would be considered for jobs on the nationals; now you do your time in the provinces and then have to give up your full-time job to work as a 'casual', doing 'shifts' – a day's work at a time, on a freelance basis – for as long as it takes until a newsdesk offers you something more permanent.

No matter how big the jumps you have made before – from a tiny weekly to a specialism on a big-city evening or from student media to regional morning paper – this will be the biggest of the lot. The daily run-of-the-mill stories will be at least the equivalent of the front-page splash in some of your previous titles. The newsrooms are also likely to be far bigger than you're used to, the executives fiercer, the hours more antisocial, the standards higher.

Quite how testing the experience will prove to be depends on where you end up working. The tabloids are generally considered a tougher, brasher stamping ground, as they are tougher, brasher papers. But the title which has the most fearsome reputation as a demanding devourer of eager young journalists is not the *Sun* or the *News of the World* but the *Daily Mail*. It is renowned for exacting executives, an admirable obsession with detail and emphasis on excellence in all aspects of journalism. It devotes time and money to stories – an all too rare approach these days. The satisfactory result, as far as all journalists who enjoy having their skills cherished are concerned, is probably the success story of the past five years. The *Daily Mail*'s circulation has risen by close to a third since 1990 and, with the closure of *Today*, went past the 2 million mark, rapidly closing on the once powerful *Mirror*.

The *Mail*'s pre-eminence and the reasons for it mean that it is one of the more likely places where newcomers to the nationals might end up working. It is one of the papers regularly on the look-out for new talent from the regions – from both news agencies and provincial papers.

The first step towards working for the *Mail*, or for any national title, is to write to the news or sports editor or chief sub with a CV and probably some cuttings. There might be a specific paper for which you want to work, but don't apply only to that one: a single letter is unlikely to be enough. Write to all the titles you would work for – perhaps every single national, perhaps just the tabloids, perhaps only the mid-market titles and the broadsheets.

If any of the executives are suitably impressed, they will probably arrange an interview and maybe a first casual shift. No matter how well it goes, you are unlikely to get a job just like that. The very best-case scenario is that a short-term contract, most likely of six months, will be offered. It is far more likely, however, that the offer will be for more shifts. You might try to fit them in over a weekend or take holiday from your full-time job to moonlight for a week. If the newsdesk still like what they see, they might offer some more shifts, again to be fitted in around your day job in the regions. You might work Monday to Friday as normal, then head to London for two shifts, one on Saturday and another on Sunday, and back to work again on Monday.

This could go on for months. You could spend all your spare time squeezing shifts into weekends and exhausting your holiday allocation without ever getting further than being offered even more shifts. At some point a decision has to be made: a full-time commitment to the nationals – resigning a job (secure, with regular pay and hours) to devote all your time to shifting (precarious, variable income from week to week and highly unpredictable, often antisocial, hours) – or not.

No national is likely to make any promises about the number of shifts it can offer. But if one indicates a couple each week, there is scope to make the move. Each shift is worth between £80 and £120, depending on the title, the day and the time it is worked. Doing two a week would bring in enough money to survive. And with scores on offer, you should be able to get more than two shifts, possibly by working for two or more papers (or radio and television stations, which also employ casuals to do behind-the-scenes research). One general rule of thumb is: try to find one Sunday and one daily to work for, to make sure of work throughout the week (including a Saturday stint for one of the Sunday titles, which are often the best payers).

If you manage to find work five days a week, you could be earning about £500. It is even possible, although not for long, to work perhaps ten or more shifts a week, earning more than £1,000, by doing a morning shift for breakfast TV and sleeping for a couple of hours in the day before doing an afternoon or evening shift for a paper. But bear in mind it can take months before shifts lead to anything more permanent. You could be exhausted very quickly.

It is generally the later reporting shifts, the ones that staffers hope to avoid, which are allocated to casuals. On the Sunday papers that will mean the Saturday-evening watches, covering any big exclusives in rival titles. On the dailies, meanwhile, they will range from the afternoon-to-evening shifts, such as 3 p.m. to 10 p.m. or 4 p.m. to 11 p.m., to the graveyard ones, covering from when everyone else is preparing to clock off until the early hours of the morning (6 p.m. to 2 or 3 a.m.). On the earlier shifts you will be covering the breaking news of the day, mostly from copy received via the computer system from the myriad freelance agencies nationwide, or getting reaction quotes and/or background to stories being prepared by other reporters, probably staffers who have been in since 10 a.m. On the later ones you will be working on breaking news, particularly from the first editions of the rival titles which are delivered to every paper's office from 10 p.m. onwards, or research to develop or write stories not for immediate use.

THE TABLOIDS, TIMING AND TAX

The Tabloids
Research, for news reporters, might include digging into the convoluted family background of a lottery winner or trying to discover a star's whereabouts after another paper splashes on some alleged misdemeanour. For most shifts are on the tabloids. A paper such as the *Mail* might have two dozen slots to be filled each week; the *Guardian* regularly has only two or three, the *Independent* even fewer and *The Times* none at all.

The reason for this is partly financial – in general broadsheets do not have the budgets to spend hundreds of thousands of pounds a year on casuals – but also journalistic: they also do not need to have legions of staff ready to stand on a doorstep waiting for a naughty celebrity's return or chasing relatives and friends of the latest victim or perpetrator of juvenile crime. If they do run such stories, they are most likely to use copy from agencies and get staffers to develop and rewrite it. Tabloid executives might argue that the broadsheets therefore fail their readers by not delivering the very latest news and comprehensive coverage of it; their broadsheet equivalents would say they concentrate on providing the stories their readers want, which are not the same as the tabloids' in content, detail or style.

The mantra of journalism – there is no right way or wrong way to develop a career – applies equally at national level. The route to your dream job, in news, sport or subbing, might be a circuitous one. It might involve spells working on tabloids when you want to be on broadsheets or vice versa, working in news when you want to be in features or sport, or in print when your desire is to be on TV. But as long as you get something out of the initial posts which helps you to the latter, they are worthwhile. Just as being a local paper reporter proves that you can write a story at any level, a stint on a national tabloid, for example, when you want to be on a broadsheet or in broadcasting will show you can survive in the toughest environment, honing the basic skills to the highest standards in the most competitive arena in journalism. No broadsheet or broadcaster is going to think that's a weakness. You can – and people do – move from the *Sun* or the *Mirror* to *The Times* or the *Guardian*, or into radio or television.

Timing

No matter who you are hoping to work for, there are two points to be made about the timing of any move to London. First, although anyone can give shifting a try, it is perhaps best done when you are young – under thirty. Then you will probably have enough experience to interest the executives but not the commitments, such as a mortgage or even a family, which could be adversely affected if your uncertain new career move falls flat. There is also an increasing trend towards youth. Piers Morgan, editor of the *Mirror*, was only in his late twenties when appointed to the top job at the *News of the World* (so becoming the youngest editor of a national this century). One of his former star columnists, showbiz writer Kate Thornton, was barely in her twenties when she was first appointed, while there are several contributors to other titles, only now around her age then, who are veterans of five years' standing or more. The only evidence pointing in the opposite direction came from London College of Printing research, which put the median age of mid-1990s national news journalists at thirty-eight, compared to thirty-four and a half, according to a 1977 survey. But, with increased openings (many on new television channels) for journalists straight out of college, the next LCP survey will almost certainly record a drop.

Second, any move is best made in the late spring or early summer. It is the period when there is most demand for casual work, for one simple reason: staff reporters go on holiday. Arriving in London by perhaps May, and being known to a few newsdesks, should be a reasonable guarantee of work. By being in the capital, close to the offices, desks can call on the day they find they have a shortage of staff and summon you in. Obviously you cannot work at such short notice if you are hundreds of miles away and have got a full-time job to worry about.

Such calls might come every day of the week. But when you are shifting you are rarely off duty, even if you want to be. You cannot turn down work without the very best excuse. You might get away with one refusal, but regular ones will lead to the calls drying up: the shifts will have gone to someone who will work every time there is a call. Some desks go a stage further and make the rather unreasonable demand that you shift only for them. It is probably best to say yes as long as they are offering some sort of guarantee of three or four shifts a week (which might mean in reality that you are called in seven days a week), but make sure that you ascertain what the chances are of getting a short-term contract. If they are keen enough on you to ask you to turn down work, they might show it and sign you up on contract (albeit after several months' shifting).

Tax

A contract means you are taken from the day-to-day existence of a casual and moved to being on the general rota as if you were staff. You will be pencilled in for shifts as before, but they are more likely to be on days than nights and you will have a guarantee of work for three, six or twelve months. You will not have all the benefits of being on staff: sick pay, pension rights and holiday time. You will remain in effect self-employed, although this is an area of some confusion. Many employers will deduct your tax from your pay, as if you were staff, even when you are doing just one casual shift. This should not happen. As a freelance you should be paid in full and be responsible for your own tax affairs.

The NUJ produces an advice guide for freelances covering tax and other common problems. It also has a London freelance section, which produces its own newsletter. The latter gives a list of what various employers pay for shifts and for stories which you might sell – for you might well try to sell stories, for example, to magazines or broadsheets while you are shifting for the tabloids. There are dozens of magazines looking for stories (for example, women's, sport and music) and if it's written by reporters who can produce good, clean, accurate copy (there are many freelances who can't) and are reliable and enthusiastic, they will soon be only too keen to employ the writers on some basis. The beauty of shifting is it can give you freedom to pursue interests which perhaps were stifled in a purely news job by working for a range of publications; the danger is that you can end up working every waking hour if you are not careful. The key is to manage and plan your time. Do not stretch yourself too far.

The same warning applies to finances when freelancing or shifting. Unlike in a staff job, you will not have a fixed income. One week you might earn £1,000, the following week £100. You will also have outgoings you probably will not have had before: a mobile telephone (which some papers will insist upon), a car (which, equally, some papers demand), a personal pension, a computer and perhaps a tax bill. Trying to break into the nationals can be stressful enough without having to work every day just to keep the bank manager happy. So keep outlays to a minimum and plan ahead, at least until you know how your efforts are going to be rewarded.

THE PRESS ASSOCIATION AND OTHER NATIONALS

Working at a national level does not have to mean working for the national papers. There is a news agency – the Press Association (PA) – which covers news countrywide and has reporters on the biggest stories of the day, every day. There are also many magazines which have a hard-news edge and are only too eager for competent, trained news reporters. These are not the more feature-orientated monthly titles such as *Cosmopolitan* or *Loaded* – although they too will hire reporters with a news background, or use them as freelances, if they feel they can do the job – but weekly titles, particularly women's magazines (see below).

The London-based PA is essentially a non-publishing newspaper which is run for, and owned by, 'real' newspapers. Its shares are owned by a mixture of national and regional newspapers groups – that is, the clients it serves (and has done for almost 130 years). It employs in its news operation around 120 journalists, who file scores of stories to give comprehensive coverage of any given day's events in Britain. (There are other agencies which perform a similar function for foreign news.) The titles it serves dip in and out of the service to report events they have not been able to attend or to receive first news of breaking stories. With reporters spread throughout the country – in twenty cities – and across the spectrum of specialisms, the breadth of coverage is unrivalled.

NATIONAL TRAINEESHIPS

For budding journalists, PA offers an alternative route into the profession – and at its highest level. Each year the agency takes a handful of trainees and puts them through a two-year training programme. It involves not classroom learning or lectures but a stint as a junior reporter, just as at scores of local papers, following a college course. In essence it is the equivalent of the standard pre-entry route. The difference is at PA you will be covering national, or even international, news rather than the more parochial events to which a local paper trainee might be assigned.

Each year about five new PA news trainees are taken on, as well as perhaps one or two at PA Sport, based in Leeds. Most are recruited from a single course: the University of Central Lancashire's NCTJ-approved postgraduate one. PA executives visit the college, sift through applications and interview candidates before inviting certain students for a placement. If that works out well, a traineeship might follow. There are, however, opportunities for budding reporters from other sources (although all must be graduates). Harry Aspey, editorial manager at PA, said, 'Other people can win places, but they are exceptions rather than the rule. They have to have written very good letters, have excellent degrees and perhaps have done some shorthand. In short, if they impress us, they will be taken on.'

The number of entrants on the news scheme varies from year to year, depending on market conditions and the need for new staff. But the operation of the scheme doesn't. Each trainee will spend time in the newsroom, working on the financial news for the City desk, at Westminster, in features and even subbing at PA's teletext service. They are paid less than full-time staffers, but a good wage, of about £14,000, by junior reporter standards. It will be increased after one year and again after two, when the trainees are considered fully fledged senior reporters.

There are also other openings for new reporters who want to work on the nationals. In recent years several titles have recruited trainees, either for in-house training schemes or from one of the more prestigious postgraduate colleges, to begin work immediately as a reporter. There are advantages for both sides: the papers hire (cheaply) new reporters, possibly the stars of the future (and also ones with a knowledge of youth culture, which can be an important factor); the young journalists start at the top – but also, sometimes quite quickly, finish there, as many of the schemes offer no guarantee of a job at the end of a fixed term or prove too tough for the aspiring reporters.

The only one which does come with a guaranteed job is run

by the *Financial Times*. Like the others mentioned below, it is aimed solely at graduates. Several hundred candidates apply for the two places on offer each year. Assistant managing editor Martin Nielsen stresses the paper is not just looking for economics specialists: 'There are lots of general reporting staff at the *FT*, so we are looking for all-rounders.' The successful two are sent to the Editorial Centre in Hastings for initial training before spending up to two years moving from department to department on the paper and on to the staff.

The other nationals which offer traineeships run their schemes on a similar basis. Both *The Times* and the *Express* are looking only for graduates. Some of the successful applicants have also done a postgraduate journalism course. Those who haven't are taught the rudiments either at a course (*The Times*) or in house (the *Express*) before rejoining their colleagues and again moving from department to department for two years. Neither scheme guarantees a job, but as *The Times*'s scheme's administrator, Elaine Jones, says, 'We can't guarantee a staff post, but so far we have been able to place everyone. After all, we have invested quite a lot in them by then.'

All three schemes have run for about eight years. Other papers, such as the *Sunday Times*, have launched similar schemes but dropped them. Others still, such as the *Independent*, once offered bursaries – including placements, which sometimes led to jobs or contracts – to journalism students, but have now stopped. The Scott Trust continues to fund bursaries for those who have already won places at City University. The scheme includes work experience at the *Guardian* but with no guarantee of a job. As you will have gathered by now, those kinds of guarantee on the nationals are very infrequent.

If you still want to try to start with a national paper, contact names and addresses for the schemes above are listed in Appendix B. Among them is a scheme run by Reuters, an international equivalent of PA, which is also described further in Chapter 6. Given that other titles might launch schemes, it is probably best to write to them too to see what they are offering. But be prepared for the fiercest of recruitment battles.

One alternative is to ask if they are looking for any researchers. But it may be that a spell writing about those washeteria break-ins might be of more practical use and stand you in better stead long-term.

SCOTLAND

Of course, there are more nationals than those already discussed. Scotland, Wales and Northern Ireland each have a national press in addition to the titles that could legitimately be described as being the London-based British nationals. In Wales there is a national morning and Sunday title as well as city evenings, in Northern Ireland two province-wide dailies and a Sunday paper.

But it is Scotland where there is the greatest non-London national press – and the most localised versions of the London titles. The last couple of years have seen a headlong rush into Scotland by the likes of the *Sun* and the *Daily Mail*. There was already the *Daily Record*, a sister publication to the *Daily Mirror*, as well as the Scottish national dailies, the Edinburgh-based *Scotsman* and Glasgow-based *Herald*, and weeklies, *Scotland on Sunday*, the *Sunday Mail* (unrelated to the English Mail group) and the *Sunday Post*. Now there are also Scottish editions of almost every 'English' title, varying in the degree of tartanisation but all aimed squarely at north of the border.

The Scottish editions sell well – for example, the *Mail* has a circulation of 119,000, the *Express* 117,000. Yet their sales are a fraction of those of the mass-market Scottish titles: the *Sunday Post*, which sells 875,000, and the *Sunday Mail*, which sells 846,000. Part of the reason for such success, and the generally healthy state of the Scottish press, are the cultural and historical differences between England and Scotland. But those differences have important consequences as far as journalists are concerned: different legal and local government systems, and therefore different training requirements for trainees.

Every one of the twenty or so NCTJ-approved colleges in England and Wales teach the same curriculum. The four in Scotland don't. They teach the Scottish varieties. But not only is course content different; so are the courses available. There is no college with a one-year pre-entry course for non-graduates. Instead there is one teaching a one-year post-graduate course and two offering two-year courses leading to a Higher National Diploma. There is also one university degree course available (full details are given in Appendix B).

Graduates of these courses are not limited to Scotland for ever – just as NCTJ-trained journalists, many of them Scots who came south to train in the days before a range of courses were available at home, can and do work in Scotland. In both cases it is purely a question of learning the differences between the two legal and council systems. But if you have done it once, you can do it twice.

WOMEN'S MAGAZINES

There are still more nationals which demand news journalists: women's magazines. Titles such as *Cosmopolitan* and *Marie Claire* are actually internationals, with different editions in different countries under the same masthead. But news journalists are more likely to be found in the less *Absolutely Fabulous* world of weekly women's magazines.

There are now more than ten such titles, ranging from the originators, such as *Woman* and *Woman's Own*, to the new launches, such as *That's Life* and *Eva*. They sell in large volumes – up to 1 million copies a week. They are mainly feature-led, but not features in the newspaper sense. Their stock-in-trade stories are newsy, human-interest ones: real-life tales of relationship break-ups or crime, the type of stories that the mid-market tabloids would – and do – follow up to put in their women's sections.

One of the most common routes into women's magazines, if not the most common, is from provincial newspapers. News reporters and, more often, feature writers or women's editors (both with news backgrounds and training, however) regularly move to London. The style of writing may be vastly different and the finished product too (glossy magazine versus local newspaper), but the basic training – the reporting and writing skills – are exactly the same on both. It is what women's magazine editors demand from long-standing staff and new recruits alike: an all-round knowledge, including law. And once you are in on a national magazine, a whole new market of potential new jobs opens up for you: moves to other weeklies, transfers to the more fashion-led monthlies (which may be less newsy but still relish candidates with a news background for their features departments) and freelancing for either or both.

With the advent of sections such as the *Daily Mail*'s Femail, there is also scope to end up on national newspapers from a local paper news background, but without passing through a national newsroom. Just as papers often hire specialists in health or the media from trade magazines, so they recruit specialists in women's features from women's magazines. You could easily go from a local paper to a national women's magazine and then to a national newspaper. And, as has already been mentioned, there is an increasing trend for magazine executives to move to newspapers at the highest levels. You might land a job as features editor on a women's magazine before transferring to take up a similar job on a paper.

Again, the key is to get your basic training on a local paper (women's magazines do not generally take trainees) and then decide where it might take you. It could be almost anywhere.

Graeme Smith, aged thirty-one, is a reporter on the *Daily Record*, one of the national papers published in Scotland. He trained on Cardiff University's NCTJ-accredited postgraduate course and worked in England before heading back to his homeland.

The whole reason people like me went to Cardiff and courses like it – and 20 per cent of those on my course were Scots – was because at that time there were no similar Scottish courses. Now that is changing, which must be good.

About half of the Scots on the course came back immediately to get jobs here, but the problem with that was the first thing they had to do was sweet-talk their employers into sending them on a conversion course to learn about the different law and local government.

I didn't come straight back, and when I did I think it was easier to understand the differences purely because I'd been a journalist for six or seven years and was quite comfortable with stories about the legal and local government systems. Perhaps if I'd come straight from college to a totally different system, it would have been more difficult.

I worked on the *Derby Evening Telegraph* for two and a half years, then moved to the *Newcastle Journal*, first as a reporter; then I moved on to the newsdesk and eventually became news editor. I came back to Scotland and shifted for a while – and now is a good time to do it because there is plenty of work.

I knew I wanted to work for the nationals, but didn't really fancy London. The advantage of Scotland is that you can do work for national papers and not have to move to London. And the titles here are quite widely respected and read in London anyway.

The other advantage is that it is quite well-paid compared to the regional press in England. I earn more now as a reporter than I did as a head of a department of twenty-five people in Newcastle – and the cost of living is cheaper compared to London.

There is also lots of work. You can come up and, if you're reasonably experienced, earn a good living. You certainly don't have to be Scottish: if you're a safe pair of hands, you'll be in demand, especially with all the tartanised versions of the English papers expanding and looking for staff.

At the moment Scotland's quite a happening place to be, in terms of the newspaper industry. Most of the London papers, especially the tabloids, have their own editions: the Scottish *Sun* even has a thistle on the masthead and supports the SNP, while others just have slip pages. It shows there's plenty of competition and demand for stories – and reporters.

Broadcast News

There has been a revolution in print journalism in the past decade or so. But it is as nothing compared to the upheaval in broadcasting. Over a slightly longer period – perhaps from the 1970s, when real journalists were replacing 'presenters' on news bulletins – television and radio stations have not only undergone massive technological and presentational changes but have also multiplied many times over.

In the past ten years the number of commercial radio stations has quadrupled to almost 200. There have been new national stations such as Virgin and Classic FM, while the BBC has also launched a new national station, Radio Five. Television has undergone equally radical changes since the day in 1982 when Channel Four was launched. Channel Five recently joined it in a ratings battle which now also includes numerous satellite and cable channels, all of which will soon be swamped by hundreds of digital non-satellite ones. The introduction of such digital terrestrial channels is already being described as the biggest change to the TV landscape since the switch from black and white to colour thirty years ago.

Some things never change, though: the need for news on many, if not all, channels; and the need for journalists to produce and package it. The total number of broadcast news journalists is almost bound to increase from the present population of an estimated 7,300. At present a third work in terrestrial TV (BBC regional or national, ITN and commercial ITV stations), just over a fifth in local radio and just under a fifth in each of national radio and other radio (predominately the BBC World Service). The remaining 10 per cent are in non-terrestrial TV or are bi-media journalists (a recent invention, most used at the BBC, whereby staff work in television *and* radio, producing reports for both). But this last sector is likely to take a far higher share of the total in the future.

As a result of the explosion in broadcast output, new specialised jobs (such as those for bi-media correspondents) and the introduction of state-of-the-art technology, training for broadcast journalists has also undergone radical changes – and is about to see more. In the early days of broadcasting, radio and then television news journalists did essentially the same job as ones in print. Often they had come from print. The technical know-how was grafted on to trained reporters or dealt with by experts who understood the intricacies of the electronics. That has become less and less the case, and will become even rarer as the concept of multi-skilling – that is, for example, one person being camera operator, sound engineer and reporter on any one story – becomes ever more common.

Today many broadcast journalists still have a print background: between 10 and 20 per cent have an NCTJ or NVQ print qualification, indicating they at least trained, and have almost certainly worked, as newspaper reporters. But there are many more courses specialising in broadcast journalism than ever before and a body equivalent to the NCTJ – the Broadcast Journalist Training Council (BJTC) – covering them. With the introduction of journalism degrees, many with a broadcast component, the chances of a broadcast journalist moving straight into radio or television without doing a stint in newspapers are growing.

But once again it is worth repeating the mantra: there is no right or wrong way into any type of journalism. Just your way.

EXTRA QUALITIES, EXTRA QUALIFICATIONS

To become a broadcast journalist you will need to be even more determined than to become a print one. Because there are perhaps a third or even 50 per cent fewer positions and because of the 'sexiness' of the subject – of which the plethora of media studies courses is evidence – competition to become a trainee, get on a training course or even land a lowly position as a freelance researcher is possibly the fiercest of all for media jobs. For example, a week after the BBC advertised it had twenty-one traineeships to fill in 1997, the recruitment department was swamped by around 10,000 requests for application forms.

Extra determination is just one of the additional qualities required, however. It should go without saying that all of these are on top of the general qualities described in the introduction. If you want to work in radio or television, you will also have to have a good, clear speaking voice. And if you want to be on screen, you might have to pass some sort of informal screen test to assess if you look right on camera. Most of all, you will almost certainly have to be a graduate.

The most common qualification for broadcast journalists is a degree: two-thirds have one, although only 5 per cent have one in journalism or featuring a journalism component. The percentage of graduates is even higher in certain subsections of broadcasting: for example, 72 per cent in national radio and 68 per cent in terrestrial TV. A quarter of all broadcast journalists have a postgraduate qualification in journalism, while almost another 20 per cent have a postgraduate qualification in another subject.

Despite the often repeated claims about tabloid TV and the 'dumbing down' of culture thanks to TV's supposedly less serious news values, broadcasters are the most highly educated of all journalists. Even those without postgraduate qualifications or degrees have some sort of qualification. More than 20 per cent of broadcast journalists have a non-degree qualification, in the majority of cases an NCTJ one. Most of the remainder have a similar qualification from the BJTC.

THE BROADCAST JOURNALISM TRAINING COUNCIL AND SKILLSET

Until recently called the National Council for the Training of Broadcast Journalists, the BJTC was initially established in the early 1980s. Comprising representatives of both the employers and the NUJ, its aim was to monitor the growing number of courses being launched for would-be broadcasters.

The difference between the NCTJ and the BJTC is that the former in effect provides training via approved colleges, while the latter monitors the training being offered by such colleges. The BJTC has no hands-on role: it doesn't set exams or play any direct part in the training process *per se*. It merely recognises college courses which reach the required standard for the industry. A decade ago eleven colleges were approved; now the number is fourteen (and will rise further). Once there were about fifteen students at each, making a total of 150 would-be broadcasters trained under the auspices of the BJTC each year; now there are more than 400.

That is a minute fraction of the 32,000 students that BJTC chairman Tom Beesley says graduate from media-related courses each year, many of them hoping to win jobs in the news side of the media. 'We are concerned how they think they are going to get a job,' he says. 'If you have that situation, you need to have some guarantee of the courses which will provide the training that students need to get into the industry and that teach what the industry needs. That is our sole role: to monitor the quality of courses.' The council doesn't claim the courses it recognises are the only way to train as a broadcast journalist, but the approval of an independent and industry-led outside body is a vital guarantee to students of complete and practical training.

Most BJTC-approved courses are one-year, full-time postgraduate ones. At present there is one intensive twenty-five-week course, again postgraduate, which runs over the summer months at the University of Central England in Birmingham, and several degree courses. Many more will no doubt follow in coming years. (For up-to-the-minute information, contact the BJTC. Its address and those of its approved colleges are listed in Appendix B.) Each concentrates on teaching radio journalism skills (although many include television segments, which is an important factor to look for when considering any course) for the simple reason that it remains the case that the majority of people starting in broadcasting work in radio first. Almost 60 per cent start at the BBC – and although the precise split between radio and television is unknown, it is a fact that the majority are in radio – and another 15 per cent in commercial radio. Another 11 per cent start in independent television, with the remainder elsewhere.

All the above statistics come from Skillset, a body with an even shorter life than the BJTC. It was launched in 1993 to promote and develop training throughout the broadcast, film and video industries. Its remit is far wider than just broadcast news journalism, but it plays a key role within the topic, liaising with the BJTC, conducting research – such as the detailed survey from which the facts above came – and developing and awarding NVQs/SVQs. Most usefully for aspiring broadcast journalists, it produces a careers guide (as does the BJTC) which is clear, comprehensive and informative (see Appendix B for addresses to obtain both it and the BJTC's). It fails, however, to cover the entire media but still would be a valuable aid to anyone looking for more detail on the intricacies of a broadcasting career.

JOURNALISM DEGREES AND STUDENT AND COMMUNITY RADIO

One of the key features of the journalism degrees – *not* media studies – which have started in the 1990s is that they give a comprehensive education including both print and broadcasting. Some of the more recent degree courses – for example, Nottingham Trent University's BJTC-approved one – are even more practical for those who are determined to work in radio or television because that is their sole topic of study. Such specialism can give you an advantage. Tom Beesley says: 'If you have a degree in broadcast journalism, you will have had three years' experience compared to a year's if you have done a postgraduate course. I think it might well be that such degree courses will become more common and popular because of that.'

But doing a degree in another subject need not hold you back. As well as the postgraduate training courses on offer, another way of getting experience while you are a student is via campus radio stations. Overseas, particularly in America, such stations have long been a vibrant presence alongside other commercial stations – and ones which also give keen and enthusiastic semi-professionals the chance to try broadcasting. It seems the same may be about to happen in this country. Already one student radio station, Oxygen FM in Oxford, has won a full-time broadcasting licence, the first student set-up to be allowed to do so. About 300 volunteers, co-ordinated by five full-time staff, are supported by one of the bigger radio stations, GWR, which is helping with training. A second operating on similar principles, in Liverpool, is hoping to achieve the same success in getting a commercial licence. It is thought more and more stations will follow suit.

The aim of providing a service is twinned with a second ambition: to train young broadcasters or at least give them basic experience and airtime. With professional broadcasting or media companies often keen to help, these stations could increasingly be the first step in a broadcasting career. Other small-scale broadcasters, such as the 100-odd community radio stations or hospital radio stations, could equally provide your first taste of on-air journalism. You will not get the formal qualifications you will need to pursue a career in broadcasting from them, but the key commodity all of the smaller-scale broadcasters offer is hands-on experience, and that sort of practice – plus the effort and determination it takes to gather it – is vital to winning places on 'official' training courses.

JOB TITLES AND MULTI-SKILLING

Not only will it look good on any application form or CV, but work experience, in whatever environment, will also give you a taste of the profession. You will learn about the technology used to produce broadcasts and the roles of those producing it. Essentially the set-up in a radio newsroom is the same as that in a newspaper. Television is no different. The reporters' role is the same, as are those of the news editor and the newsdesk generally. The news-gathering operation – from the news diary to district offices – is the same. The difference, obviously, lies in the production side. The equivalent of newspaper subs in radio are, approximately, the editors and producers, approximately because there is a lot more emphasis on self-subbing in broadcasting, a trend which will become more pronounced as 'multi-skilling' (see below also) takes a firmer hold.

The other chief differences between print and broadcasting are also obvious: style and technology. Radio journalists have to be on the look-out for audio garnishes for a story; their television equivalents, visual ones. The 'soundbites' or pictures have to be worked into the story to bring it to life, otherwise broadcast news bulletins might as well involve someone sitting behind a microphone reading out a newspaper report.

New technology makes the task of electronic news gathering easier – and more complicated. Lightweight cameras and tape recorders, not to mention the satellite communication of material, means news can be on screens or airwaves more quickly than ever before and in a clearer form. Once if a story occurred on the other side of the world, it would take days for any pictures of it to be seen. Now, to use one recent example, when yachtsman Tony Bullimore capsized thousands of miles from anywhere television was carrying images of the upturned hull within hours. But such advances also mean the technical expertise needed by reporters is greater than before.

All the buzz words in broadcasting now stress the need to adopt a flexible approach to such technology. Working practices are shifting to embrace it. Bi-media correspondents are expected to be *au fait* with both TV and radio. At the BBC the demarcation lines between reporters and producers are being eroded so that staff have the catch-all title of 'broadcast journalists' and are expected to act as both reporters or producers as needed. The ethos has reached its peak with the development of video journalists (VJs) – described in more detail below – reporters who not only report but also shoot the film to accompany it and edit the package.

There are now entry-level openings for VJs. There is even talk of courses teaching the subject being established. Such schemes sit alongside the more traditional in-house training schemes offered by the BBC and ITN. But for many budding broadcast journalists who have gone through the college system, such a Jack- or Jill-of-all-trades approach is equally often a necessity in their first jobs – in local radio.

THE EMPLOYERS

LOCAL RADIO AND TELEVISION

Multi-skilling was invented in local radio – and for a very simple reason. 'People with small budgets, lots of airtime to fill and a talented and enthusiastic team of people will inevitably "make do", each helping another to develop and apply new skills,' as Skillset puts it. 'To be successful in local radio, people need to be able to turn a hand to most things . . . with a smile.'

Local radio in this instance really means commercial local radio. The BBC has forty-two local stations but they are outnumbered by 150 or so commercial rivals. These are the stations which have been at the sharp end of multi-skilling because their budgets have often been the tightest – pay in commercial local radio is among the lowest of any sector of the media, according to the NUJ. It has one of the highest proportions of employees earning under £10,000 (a fifth) and only a quarter earning £25,000 or above. In comparison, only 7.3 per cent of BBC local radio employees were on under £10,000 and almost half earned £25,000 or more.

What money can't buy you, however, if you want to make your way into broadcasting, is the experience of working at local level. Just as in newspapers now, there are chances to enter the broadcasting arm of journalism as a trainee at national level (see below). But, again just as in newspapers, you can join at the bottom and work your way up – however far that might be – while enjoying perhaps a broader professional education. The basics you learnt at the lower level may even open your eyes to wider horizons within broadcasting. For example, the comedian Chris Morris – whose parodies of news programmes have earned him both fame and infamy – was once a news reporter on BBC Radio Bristol. His former boss while he was at Radio One, station controller

Matthew Bannister, is also an ex-journalist. He started on BBC Radio Nottingham and was a Radio One news reporter years before becoming the station's boss.

Both, like all broadcasters with their background, will have learnt not only to gather the news – from interviewing to story spotting – and to report, edit and present it but also to think on their feet in order to develop stories and programmes. Like all local radio reporters, they will have covered 'hard' news stories, such as accidents and politics, but will also have conducted vox pops and recorded lighter items. In short, they will have received a similar all-encompassing grounding as local newspaper reporters, some of whom may eventually become colleagues on the stations.

Such switching between print and broadcast journalism is generally done at a local level. It is rarer to find a reporter, or any other type of journalist, who breaks through to the higher levels of the press and then moves into radio or television. The route is more likely to be one in which a news reporter on a local paper, probably a daily, will be recruited to join a radio station and then perhaps on to TV. Alternatively, a specialist on a paper might be recruited into television – or, more likely today, to a bi-media post – to cover the same topic as a specialist broadcast reporter. For example, Robin Oakley, the BBC's political editor, was recruited from *The Times*. Once again the range of career paths is as numerous as the thousands of people in the profession.

IRN AND ITN

The bulletins on most commercial radio stations follow national news reports from Independent Radio News (IRN). It is, unsurprisingly, the radio arm of International Television News (ITN), the company which provides news for Channels Three, Four and Five. IRN employs just under fifty journalists at its London offices to provide news for Classic FM and 128 local stations, while ITN has more than 600 staff, including more than 130 journalists for its main service, almost sixty for Channel Four News and almost sixty for Channel Five News.

Many of these national reporters will have followed a route

similar to that of their colleagues in the national press: starting in local journalism before moving ever upwards and arriving in London. They are less likely to have had to shift, as such a system is mostly absent from broadcasting. They will have been recruited into jobs via advertisements. But these might not be full-time staff jobs. One of the characteristics of the media in the 1990s, and especially broadcasting, is the widespread use of contracts. According to the NUJ, the overall ratio of staffers to contract workers is 10:1. But in broadcasting two-thirds are on staff, while 19 per cent are on contracts of a year or more and 8 per cent on contracts of less than a year, all according to Skillset.

Many IRN/ITN journalists have joined the company another way: via its graduate training schemes (the address for application is given in Appendix B). Each year one radio trainee and between four and six television trainees are recruited to undergo an in-house scheme. Competition is fierce: in 1996 the successful four candidates for the TV scheme were chosen from 3,200 applicants. And their qualifications before they even started the in-house training were impressive: one had a BJTC postgraduate diploma in journalism (as had another four of the unsuccessful shortlisted candidates), one had an MA in documentary television following on from a drama, film and television degree, another an MA in TV film and production and the final one a degree in politics, philosophy and economics from Oxford University.

All of them, just like many of the faces on the screens today who have undergone the same training, spend six months in a classroom learning the basics of journalism, such as the law, and of broadcasting techniques and technology. The following year is spent in the field, working on various programmes as journalists but overseen by editors and other trainers. At the end of the eighteen months they move on to the staff as fully fledged journalists. Martin Hurd, director of resources at ITN, says, 'If they get to eighteen months, we're not going to throw them away, having done all the training.' The radio scheme is similar but obviously tailored for audio only.

But, Mr Hurd says, the courses will soon undergo some changes. 'We are changing for a very, very simple reason.

When we first started these courses in the 1960s there was no such thing as broadcast training courses. When we start a course now we are finding that in the first six months we're just repeating what the trainees have done at university or college because now there are so many postgraduate courses. I have to say that if you want to be a broadcast journalist, you can do no worse than by doing one of those courses – if you can afford to.'

THE BBC

Changes have already occurred to the BBC's equivalent of the ITN graduate training schemes: all new entrants to the corporation are now trained as bi-media journalists. In one of the guides it produces it makes clear why: 'We believe that bi-media working is the way of the future. It provides an opportunity to pool the talents, skills, ideas and information of both radio and television to produce programmes of the greatest range and quality.'

News is central to the BBC's output. In the words of Tony Hall, chief executive of the corporation's News Directorate: 'Journalism of the highest quality is central to the service the BBC gives to the public. On television and radio our aim is to inform our audiences, without sensationalism, about the key issues which affect our nation.' That process is realised via the flagship news bulletins and a whole range of news and current-affairs programmes such as *Panorama* on BBC1, *Newsnight* on BBC2, *Today* on Radio Four and the entire output of the twenty-four-hour news and sport network Radio Five. In 1994/5 such programmes were part of 11,000 hours of news and current-affairs output. In any one week more than 33 million viewers tuned to BBC news programmes for thirty minutes or more.

Of course, such enormous output requires a huge number of journalists. Indeed, 10 per cent of the corporation's operating expenditure of £189 million in 1994/5 paid for more than 1,700 staff, making the BBC's national and international news operation one of the biggest in the world. In this country there are four specialist units – economics, foreign affairs, politics and social affairs – where 60 per cent of BBC journalists work. In addition there are twenty-six bi-media bureaux around the world, which, combined with the World Service, means the BBC is represented in over fifty countries.

The national, and international, news operation is known as the network news. But on top of that there is the BBC's regional broadcasting from thirteen centres, including Belfast, Birmingham, Cardiff, Glasgow, Leeds, Manchester, Norwich, Plymouth and Southampton. Each centre produces its own nightly news magazine and bulletins throughout the day. Many share premises – and staff, thanks to the introduction of bi-media correspondents – with one of the BBC's local radio stations. The corporation employs more than 2,000 journalists in its regional stations.

The two branches of the corporation, network and regional, both have openings for new blood. Each operates a training scheme, overseen by central journalist trainers. But each scheme, as mentioned above, is fantastically oversubscribed. In 1996 there were 5,000 requests for application forms for each scheme within a week of its being advertised in the *Guardian*. The network trainee scheme had eight places; the regional one thirteen.

The advertisement gave a good idea of what qualities were required: the ability to spot and tell a story, a broad knowledge of current affairs, an enquiring mind and the determination and resilience to pursue a story, among others. If anyone doubts the value of work experience, they should note another requirement contained in the advertisement: 'You will probably have had some involvement in journalism either at work, college or as a volunteer – or you will be able to show through your experience that you have the qualities needed to be a journalist.' Again, as with ITN, that increasingly means having gained a postgraduate journalism qualification.

Rhona Christie, head of BBC journalist training, adds: 'What we are looking for is a proven interest in news and current affairs and the ability to develop an argument or a story in an objective way. They will also have an investigative mind and lots of determination.' The last quality will be needed for the rigorous selection process, which starts with a demanding application form and moves on to group exercises and written tests before interviews and, eventually, final interviews. Only then – after a process which has already taken several months – does the training begin.

The regional scheme begins with four months' classroom training, the remainder of the time being spent in a region, working in radio and television. The network scheme starts with similar basic grounding – in law, BBC style and radio and television techniques – before trainees move to placements on a number of national programmes. Both schemes are bi-media-based. Increasingly, it is expected, they will become multi-media-based, with trainees also learning about teletext, the Internet and other new media. Both last a year, during which time the trainees are on contracts. At the end of them there is no guarantee of a job with the BBC, but a very high success rate of above 90 per cent. Even those without work immediately still have a great training to help them find a job.

SKY, SATELLITE AND CABLE

Sky is the most talked- and written-about satellite television station. Its domination of sports coverage, especially football, means it has been at the forefront of the dramatic changes seen in the last few years. Its money has helped transform sport, from stadia to stars' salaries. But it, and other new stations, has also been in the frontline of another revolution: that of news journalism.

Sky's contribution has been to introduce the concept of 'rolling', or twenty-four-hour, news to British television. Its dedicated news channel is there to provide both speedy news of breaking stories but also analysis and in-depth coverage of the day's events. Rupert Murdoch, Sky's major shareholder via his News International empire, has already spoken of establishing a global twenty-four-hour news service to rival America's CNN. Sky has also challenged ITN, unsuccess-fully, for the contract to provide news to the ITV stations.

But Sky in many ways is a traditional, if youthful, challenger to the BBC and ITN. For aspiring broadcast journalists, cable channels, such as Channel One and L!ve TV, are more important – first, because they offer formal trainee level entry whereas Sky does not and, second, because of the general impact they have had on training and the approach of the whole industry to the subject. Once again the key word is multi-skilling.

VJs AND MULTI-SKILLING

In this country cable television is essentially famous for two things: the news bunny and topless darts. If you are unaware of either, it is probably no great loss (although as a potential journalist perhaps you should know about them). They are the brainchild of former *Sun* editor Kelvin MacKenzie, the head of L!ve TV, and part of a strategy of moving away from the mainstream approaches to news. But it is the second part of the strategy, common to L!ve's rival cable operator Channel One as well, which is more important to budding journalists. It centres on city-based local television.

Both L!ve and Channel One have headquarters in London but offices too in the various cities where they operate: L!ve in Birmingham, Liverpool, Manchester and Edinburgh; Channel One in Liverpool and Bristol, with more promised in Leeds, Southampton and Wolverhampton, among others. Each station offers a diet of local news, usually produced in association with one of the local newspapers, as the print companies are often partners in the cable enterprises. More than 1.5 million homes in the country have access to cable, and the Newspaper Society has described cable as 'perhaps the most attractive alternative' to local newspapers in the future, although the 'potential threat is also a glaring opportunity'. Local newspaper journalists could soon regularly become TV journalists without leaving the same parent company. At present both L!ve and Channel One advertise regularly in the media sections of the national newspapers and in *Press Gazette*. L!ve generally looks for reporters and other staff with broadcast experience. Channel One, on the other hand, has pioneered a new style of presentation and presenter: the video journalist.

They are often from a newspaper background. They are

trained journalists, with experience, who are then trained to operate as broadcasters. But broadcasters with a difference: they not only report on a story but also film it and edit it back at the studio. They not only set up interviews and conduct them, but do so while holding a lightweight camera. Since its launch in November 1994, Channel One has created more than 200 jobs, a quarter of them for VJs. Now those staff are moving on and taking their multi-skilled approach elsewhere. For example, Channel Five's news is provided by several Channel One veterans.

Channel One's managing director, Julian Aston, is proud of the station's role: 'Quite simply, we are changing the UK television culture. All of the old methods and practices, so much a part of the television scene for sixty years, have been rethought by Channel One. Without the luxury of the licence fee or the vast advertising income of the well-established terrestrial broadcasters, we have had to create new ways of working in the new broadcasting age.'

The VJ concept was born in Norway and has since been copied in America, Germany and Switzerland as well as elsewhere in Europe. Its aim is to have as few internal barriers as possible, so that reporters are also producers and editors. Its disciples claim it allows greater flexibility and increased efficiency for smaller stations with a limited staff. But its appeal is likely to spread into the bigger stations. Already Ron Neil, the BBC's head of regional broadcasting, has told *Press Gazette*, 'When you look at Channel One you see the VJ doing it all and it looks very good – that mixed economy will certainly have to come into our operation.'

For the moment most VJs are already journalists who switch from print or radio to television. In the future that will change. A VJ training course, aimed at postgraduates, is due to be launched by Channel One in conjunction with City University, London. It will be the first of its kind in the country. Students will be taught, over the course of an academic year, how to write, film and edit stories. They will be formally trained as journalists, but specifically video journalists, for three days a week at college. On the remaining two they will work at Channel One, learning the practical application of their skills. They will also be able to work at the station during holidays, gaining more experience and possibly even the offer of a contract or a job. More details are available from the university (whose address is given in Appendix B).

Such openings will be highly sought after. But it is worth stressing that broadcasting, especially at the small stations or channels, is the one area where formal training courses are not the only way in. Yes, you will probably need to be trained, but it is not uncommon for trainees to be taken on from jobs working as runners or newsdesk secretaries or other administrative jobs. There is a theory that if you can get your foot in the door and be persistent, you might eventually be given your chance.

Of course, there is no guarantee. But one thing is certain: the high educational standards which are now almost compulsory to get into broadcast journalism are beginning to create a backlash. Rhona Christie, of the BBC, says, 'Part of my concern is that we are in danger of getting very middle-class entrants only. We've got to be able to recruit from across the whole of society. At the end of the day we are looking for people with good communication skills – and that doesn't necessarily mean having to have a first-class degree.'

How long before broadcasting starts seeing modern apprenticeships and NVQs, like newspapers? Again, the only advice that can be offered is to keep up with any developments via *Press Gazette* and to remember that work experience and proof you really want to be a journalist will always be as important as whatever paper qualification is needed. Determination and desire are the watchwords.

Lynne Wilson, aged twenty-nine, is a senior broadcast journalist with BBC Essex. She studied English at university, where she was also editor of the student newspaper. She attended London's City University broadcasting training course.

I started in commercial radio and I think that gave me a really good grounding. You are on your own much more, so you have to learn to do everything. You get to be well-versed in a wide range of skills and get plenty of experience.

My first job was at Radio Hallam in Sheffield, then Viking in Hull – both part of the group which gave me a bursary to go to college – and I was a year at each. I was a reporter, but because it was only a small team you got the chance to present as well and produce.

I moved to BBC Radio Northampton for just over two years, then to Essex, where I am now on the newsdesk. I also sit on the boards for recruitment and see applications as well as getting letters about jobs. I got one this morning which said, 'I am looking for a position in the areas of PR, broadcasting or marketing.' How huge an area is that? I'm afraid that's going straight into the bin. He's just after a position, any position. You have got to be determined to be a journalist and set your heart and soul on being one.

I would still say the best way in is via one of the recognised journalism courses, but one which offers a TV option, and make sure it is really up to date on the technical side. Most people who are now coming in are from courses, not from papers, and people who do come from papers are expected to have some technical knowledge – perhaps from an evening class or work experience.

But the management attitude here, and in most places, is that you can always train someone to use a tape-recorder or use a desk but it takes a lot longer to train someone as a journalist. We are looking for people who are reporters first, but obviously if you have the technical know-how as well, you have an advantage.

The key thing today is to be flexible. However you were trained or whatever you learnt on your basic course, you have to be prepared to change with the times. You have to be ready to use equipment you might not have used before and be flexible about the kind of work you do, and where you do it, because you might be sent all over the patch.

Most of all, you have to have all-round knowledge and empathy with the concerns of the listeners and what makes them tick. It's no use living in your own world and reading just one broadsheet. It's no use a presenter turning around during a live broadcast and saying, for example, 'Who's Kevin Keegan?' There's no time to brief them. They have to know.

Nikki Chadwick, aged thirty, is a programme anchor and reporter on Channel Three North-East, formerly Tyne-Tees. She attended London College of Printing's postgraduate broadcast journalism course despite not completing her degree.

I had always wanted to be a journalist and go into radio after I visited a station when I was a child. When I was a student I got work experience at my local BBC station in Lincoln and, because of that, got a place on the broadcasting course.

I got a job in commercial radio in Birmingham, then another one, and stayed there for a couple of years before I decided to go to London and do shifts in the press office at London Weekend Television. But it was at the time that the satellite station BSB had just closed down and the competition for any job anywhere was fierce. It was really pretty horrible, with everyone fighting for jobs, so I thought it was a good time to get out.

I hated PR anyway. You were not doing the job you came into journalism to do. You were just a middle man. You couldn't produce anything of your own. You were just a spokesman for someone else, saying what they wanted you to say.

For about two years I worked in bars and doing other jobs before I ended up working for a wildlife group in Cleveland. I thought I'd try journalism again, wrote to Tyne Tees and was offered shifts, and the first time I walked into the office I got the buzz again. Once a Nosy Parker, always a Nosy Parker, I suppose.

It took a few months to get offered anything permanent, but I've been here ever since, about three years. Now I present part of the hour-long evening show nearly every night, but I also still go out reporting.

I love it because, as a journalist, you can find out about absolutely anything. The world is your oyster. There's also a whole range of places you get to go to that you wouldn't if you weren't a journalist.

A typical day starts with the news conference at 9.30 a.m. You then go out on stories, which in some ways is easier than print and in some ways more difficult. You don't have to worry about taking notes, but on the other hand you've got to think about pictures all the time. You go out with one cameraman and then get back and edit with an editor.

People do sometimes think the job is glamorous – and it is a great job to have – but it is not necessarily as glamorous as people think, especially when you're standing in the rain on a live outside broadcast. It's damned hard, although the rewards are quite good. But don't think it's easy.

Dermot Murnaghan, aged thirty-nine, is presenter of ITN's *Lunchtime News* and the documentary series *The Big Story*.

After a history degree, he freelanced before winning a place on a print journalism course. He worked on an evening paper and then became a researcher on a Channel Four programme. After specialising in business for five years, he began presenting for ITN five years ago.

When I graduated I thought, like a lot of people, I suppose, that it would be quite nice to be a journalist, having dabbled a bit at university.

I started freelancing at twenty-one or twenty-two – sending articles off to people and getting an occasional cheque for £10. But with no contacts, it was impossible. You'd also find people would say your ideas were rubbish – and then see them in print a couple of weeks later!

I decided to formalise my career and did the course at City University. It was in the early days, when the industry was changing and employers were beginning to recognise that these sorts of courses separated the wheat from the chaff.

I did the basics – shorthand, law and so on – and also did a placement at the *Coventry Evening Telegraph*, which led to a job. That's one of the advantages of those courses: you can develop contacts through placements and they can lead to jobs.

I was only there for about six months because Channel Four was launching around that time and I got a job on a business programme, first as a researcher and later presenting. From there I went on, again with changes in television, to a European satellite station. When that collapsed I got a job at ITN.

Television isn't harder than print, but it is different. Employers will look for ability and a brain rather than technical expertise. It's the basics that count – that's why local paper experience can be useful. If you can write a story, you can pick up the other skills later, and you will be given training for that.

My colleagues around the office are split between those who came straight into broadcasting and those who came from print – and *they* have greater experience: they've done the courts and have been filing stories every day. The only real difference between television and print is obvious: the need to think pictures. Otherwise writing stories is the same.

I am lucky in that I have the luxury of doing *The Big Story*, which means I have a routine type of a job presenting the news and also a less routine one in which you just don't know what you might be doing.

If I was doing it all again, I would still go through print. ITN has always had journalists, not actors or news readers, presenting the news, and now that I'm presenting, I am still writing – introductions and links – just as I was when I started out.

Working Abroad

Until recently Martin Dunn was said to be one of the best-paid editors in America. He was widely credited with saving New York's tabloid *Daily News*. But he was afforded only grudging respect in some quarters. The reason? Because he was a Brit in a city where the media were, and are, full of them – and were, and are, almost as full of resentment at their presence.

In late 1996 he announced he was returning to work in Britain again. But there is still a regular outward flow of journalistic talent. Apart from Mr Dunn, well-known media figures ranging from Harry Evans, award-winning former editor of the *Sunday Times*, to Wendy Henry, an ex-*News of the World* editor, have made new homes in the States. Other Fleet Street and provincial press veterans have moved elsewhere: Hong Kong, where ex-*Observer* editor Jonathan Fenby headed, Australia, Canada, New Zealand and just about everywhere else where English is widely spoken – and a good few places where it isn't.

One of the great advantages of journalism is that its practice is universal. Unlike other professions, where a qualification in one country may not be valid in another, reporters or subs can travel and apply their skills pretty much as they did at home. The legal or government systems may be slightly different, but essentially a story is a story whatever the niceties of judicial or civic administration. Furthermore, a British training is sometimes seen as a great advantage – whatever some people, perhaps New Yorkers, might say.

WHAT KIND OF JOB?

If you want to work abroad, there is a range of possibilities. You could build your career in Britain, rising through the ranks until you have managerial experience, and then look for similar positions overseas. This is the route that the likes of Messrs Dunn, Evans and Henry followed. It is the one mainly for Fleet Street high-fliers. Others who have followed it have worked in, for example, the Middle East or Hong Kong. Again, they have tended to be figures with managerial experience of the nationals – papers or magazines – in London.

Alternatively, your aim might be to qualify and get some reporting experience before spreading your wings. The jobs sections of both the *Media Guardian* and *Press Gazette* regularly carry advertisements for vacancies overseas. One recent example was: 'Subs wanted by the *Daily Star* in Beirut. Free flight. Free accommodation. Free sun. Free of tax.' Another: 'Vienna. A new English-language daily to be launched in the spring is looking for a news editor and three journalists.' In the news columns of *Press Gazette* there are regular reports of Brits heading abroad, editors of women's magazines being the latest growth area for emigration. Tabloid reporters and photographers also regularly depart to apply their skills to new markets. Indeed, one of America's most successful agencies is run by British expats.

You might decide to travel and work, picking a destination – or several – and aiming to secure a short-term job there or some shifts (if immigrants are allowed to do such work). You would be back at the stage of the trainee looking for a first job: deciding who you wanted to work for and writing speculative letters to them. You might leave for a new country with just the promise of a few shifts. But the move could lead you off in a new career direction – from print to broadcasting, as you discover skills you never knew you had – or offer the freedom to pick and choose how, where and when you work (for example, a couple of days a week as a TV researcher mixed with a few working as a print reporter). And if you decide you are fed up with a particular job or location, even a certain country, you can move on and try your luck somewhere else.

If you are determined to travel to work, but want to explore less well-known regions or places where being or speaking English is less vital, you might want to become a 'stringer'. You would set yourself up as a freelance reporting on overseas news to foreign desks in London or elsewhere. You could be covering breaking news from a country or issues there which have an impact elsewhere – for example, arms exports from developed countries to the Third World or sex tourism by Westerners exploiting children in the Far East. Initially at least, you would probably be working for a range of outlets: daily and Sunday papers, perhaps in several countries, as well as radio and television. In time one might offer a more permanent deal, such as a contract to write for it alone.

The next step might be a move on to the staff as a foreign correspondent. Equally, you might arrive at one of these sought-after postings from working in Britain for a paper or broadcaster with a network of overseas staff. By offering stories or undertaking your own trips, you might draw the foreign desk's attention to your potential as a correspondent which would help you develop your career overseas. Once again, there is no certain way to achieve your goal.

SKILLS

Without question one of the key skills needed to work abroad is languages. We are lucky in this country that English is one of the most widely spoken languages in the world. Not only is it the most common language in countries such as America, Australia, Canada and New Zealand but it is frequently the first foreign language spoken by many non-English-speakers. Purely because of this historical fact, British journalists have an unrivalled choice of countries where it would be possible for them to work easily.

But if you want to move away from the English-speaking parts of the world and report on other areas, you will need a foreign language. That might be French, Portuguese or Spanish, which, like English, are commonly spoken all over the world because of the former colonies each nation cultivated. Or it might be one of the languages associated with newer empires – Chinese or Russian. As these communist and ex-communist countries' relationships with the West thaw, so the numbers of journalists visiting them and reporting from them will increase.

More important for would-be foreign correspondents, though, is probably bags of determination and daring. Unlike colleagues back at home, you are unlikely to be reporting mainly on a basic news agenda. You are far more likely to be covering stories in difficult conditions, whether because of the climate, violence or harassment and suspicion of foreigners. Often, with droughts, floods or other natural disasters, the stories themselves are the difficult conditions. Add in the types of language and cultural differences which can make the simplest request a bureaucratic nightmare and you realise why relentless drive is so important.

It is also vital because it is what is needed to start off any career as a foreign correspondent. Overseas staff jobs are like gold dust. The chances of landing one just like that are nil. You might well have to initiate a move abroad yourself by getting work as a freelance – the ubiquitous stringer.

STRINGERS AND STAFF CORRESPONDENTS

No newspaper or broadcaster can cover every corner of the world with staff reporters. It is impossible, for both financial and logistical reasons, to have a reporter in every country. Instead, foreign editors control a network of correspondents located in the countries which most regularly produce news for a British market: for example, America, Russia and Belgium (because of the European Union).

Different titles and programmes within the various strands have differing levels of commitment to overseas reporting. The BBC, particularly because of the World Service but also because it is more concerned with foreign news, has many more foreign correspondents than ITN. Equally, the broadsheet papers have far more foreign staff, and stringers, than the tabloids. The *Guardian*'s and the *Observer*'s joint foreign operation consists of fourteen full-time correspondents in places such as Washington, New York, Paris, Bonn, Brussels, Rome, Moscow, Johannesburg, Jerusalem, Beirut and Hong Kong. In addition, the papers have reporters on full-time contracts in a further eight or so locations. A tabloid rival might have only one or two overseas staff, probably in America for showbiz stories.

The final layer of the broadsheets' comprehensive coverage – a network of stringers – is therefore an equally vital part of the tabloids' set-up. They are freelances but ones with a limited market, not because they are incapable of working for everyone, but because normally a stringer for the *Guardian*, for example, will not also work for competitors such as the *Independent*, the *Telegraph* or *The Times*. He or she would have an agreement with one title to put stories its way or cover what it wanted. That deal might involve a fixed monthly retainer and a small amount for each story used or just payment for stories used alone. Obviously, such deals mean a stringer has to work for more than one title: perhaps a broadsheet, a mid-market tabloid, magazines, broadcasters and non-English titles.

If you think you might want to try being a stringer, there are a few things to bear in mind. First, many places are already more than adequately covered – it's highly unlikely that anyone is going to need more correspondents in America or most of mainland Europe. You will need to identify a country or area which is poorly covered. Second, you will need to ensure that a foreign editor or two agrees with your analysis before you move abroad to your chosen venue. If they are reluctant to receive stories from that area, you will struggle from day one; finally, even if you succeed, you will not be very well paid. But money is probably not the reason you are doing it.

Simon Tisdall, the *Guardian*'s foreign editor, says the problems of setting up as a stringer mean there is a high failure rate: 'You can be very successful, but the failure rate can be very high as well. Some who talk about it never do it and don't get out there, and of those who do actually do it only about one in ten make it' (making it being winning a staff job or contract as a correspondent).

The alternative route is a domestic one: getting a job with a national newspaper or broadcaster with overseas staff and then working your way abroad. The process might involve suggesting stories to the foreign desk or volunteering to undertake a trip to cover a particular topic. And given that foreign correspondents are these days expected to contribute 'across the paper' or the schedules – that is, producing stories not only for the foreign news pages or the *Nine O'Clock News* but also for sport and arts or *Newsnight* and *Correspondent* – the all-round grounding of the newsroom can sometimes be an advantage.

REUTERS, THE WORLD SERVICE AND THE BBC

There are other ways of becoming a foreign correspondent – ways which are open to even aspiring journalists.

The first is via the news agency Reuters, one of the international equivalents of the Press Association. Each year between five and ten trainees are taken on from around 500 applicants. They are all graduates (with 2.1 degrees or better) fluent in English and at least one other language and under the upper age limit of twenty-eight. By the time they complete their training the oldest successful candidates are over thirty, as the scheme lasts two and a half years.

The trainees join the firm, which has reporters in 150 countries around the world and a total staff of 1,500, in the autumn and spend most of the period until Christmas in classrooms learning the basics before joining the office and learning on the job via attachments to various desks. By the time the summer arrives most are sent for their first overseas posting – usually in Europe but this depends on which second language the reporter speaks – lasting a year. The final six months of the scheme are spent back in London, partly so that trainees can begin to look for full-time overseas postings when the scheme ends (and when the trainees are taken on staff).

Colin McKinnon, one of the scheme's chief tutors, says there are firm ideas about who the company wants – and who they don't: 'We get lots of people who just want to travel. They think Reuters is like a travel agency which is going to send them to gallivant all over the place. It's not. It's all about journalism and good reporting.' There are also some assets potential staff should have. 'We are looking for people who are not afraid of economic and market news because business stories are a big part of the service we provide.'

The rewards for successful applicants include not just a good training and an enviable start in journalism but the potential for a long career. Many of the trainees who have completed the scheme in its thirty-year history are now senior executives at the agency.

Another, equally esteemed organisation offering openings for aspiring journalists is the BBC World Service. But it is one for which it is more difficult to give concrete guidance on how to join. Many of its journalists, numbering more than 1,000 in all, come from a domestic news background, having passed through other newsrooms in the corporation. Specific language strands, however, do have entry-level vacancies occasionally. The main qualification needed is fairly obvious: speaking the relevant language to the highest levels. Hossein Shahidi, the World Service's senior journalist trainer, says that often staff first join as translators at the BBC's monitoring station or via non-reporting jobs, such as studio managing, in one of the service's forty or so different language departments. They develop journalistic and technical skills on the job and through training courses. Approximately 150 people a year join the World Service in that way and are sent on in-house training courses.

Other BBC overseas staff report to the News and Current Affairs section to feed network bulletins and special programmes. The Foreign Affairs Unit, headed by John Simpson, the foreign affairs editor, 'reports on international events, aiming to provide a fuller understanding of world affairs'. Twenty-six bi-media bureaux around the world contribute to that mission. Taken with the World Service, as we have seen, this means that the BBC is represented in more than fifty countries, which is the largest network of foreign correspondents, it claims, of any broadcaster. Again, the route to being one of those correspondents is via the domestic news operations and, before that, one of the in-house training schemes. It can't be stressed too much that winning a place on one of them could present incredible opportunities.

Jess Carter, aged twenty-seven, is a producer with an NBC-affiliated local television station in California. She completed an NCTJ course before working on a weekly and an evening paper. In 1992 she moved to Hong Kong, where she worked in newspapers and radio, before leaving for America three years later.

I was interested in journalism from about the age of fourteen and did work experience at my local paper while I was still at school. I went to journalism college after my A-levels and worked for almost five years before deciding to go abroad.

It was a decision which came completely out of the blue. I had just been quite fed up. I remember sitting in my flat on a cold, rainy November day and thinking, 'I've had enough.' And that was that.

I got a book about working abroad and read about various places. As soon as I saw there was an English-language paper in Hong Kong, I decided to go there. I don't speak any foreign languages very well, so it had to be somewhere where English was spoken.

I decided to try to get a job as a journalist if possible, but, if not, I was happy to work in bars, see what happened and just travel. It looked like that was what would happen as I flew out without any work lined up.

But within three weeks I was subbing on a magazine, then I edited a trade magazine before getting a job on the English-language paper – by offering it a story which ended up as the front-page lead – and then going into radio.

There is a foreign correspondents' club in Hong Kong which is a massive networking environment and it was a key way of meeting people and getting on. You could be sitting next to anyone – a veteran of covering the war in Vietnam or someone fresh in from Woking – and that's the way to get work or even just work experience to get your face known.

Before I left England I wrote formal letters and people replied saying, 'There's nothing on. Don't come out.' Even if you write a formal letter when you're there, it will probably be ignored. You need to just meet people and get chatting to them.

I met my husband, who is American, in Hong Kong and left with him to go back to America, where he wanted to go to college. I had to start from scratch again – and it was harder because there is an attitude that you are taking jobs off Americans.

I worked in radio for six months and then someone asked me to produce a TV show. I'd never done it before, or even worked in television, but I just said, 'Yes.' Basically you have to grab every opportunity that comes along.

In my last six months in Hong Kong I got into radio, which I'd never done before, but if someone gives you a chance you have to say, 'Yes.' You just have to remember that you're a journalist and you're capable of doing any of these jobs.

It certainly hadn't occurred to me before I left England that I would work in radio or television. I would probably still be in newspapers if I was in England. But travelling, and especially to Hong Kong, made me realise that the world is your oyster.

Emily Buchanan, aged thirty-eight, is a BBC foreign-affairs correspondent based in London. She travels widely in India, Africa and South America as part of her brief to cover the developing world. A Sussex University history graduate, she was one of the first intake on City University's broadcasting course.

I went for an interview at City for a place on the print course, but they asked if I would be interested in a broadcasting one which they were about to start. I've been in broadcasting ever since, starting by freelancing for the BBC World Service after a couple of attachments on local radio during the course.

I worked as a producer on Radio Four before going into television and working on *Newsnight* and *On the Record*. I specialised in politics, but despite that I'd always wanted to work abroad. I've just been around the houses to get there.

Probably a more normal path would have been to have stayed as a reporter and have gone abroad and been a stringer. I'm a bit different in having a current-affairs background rather than pure news, but that is very useful because I am used to generating my own ideas.

A typical month might break down into two weeks planning a trip, coming up with ideas – you probably need two or three to make a trip worthwhile – and trying to sort out the arrangements. You might film for about a week and then edit for a week when you get back.

It is essential to have languages if you want to work abroad. I speak French and Italian, but I'd like to speak more, Spanish or Russian perhaps, languages spoken in a large area of the world. Having languages means you don't have to interview through translators or rely on them every time you need to talk to someone. It's also extremely useful, when you are trying to get through border controls, if you can chat to the guards.

A lot of people say it must be a very glamorous job, but it is actually completely unglamorous and very, very hard. When you're flying for hours, then driving for hours, often in unpleasant conditions, and then doing the same thing over and over again for perhaps ten days, going from one interview to the next, it is very gruelling. It's not like going on holiday.

It is very demanding, particularly being away from home for weeks at a time. If you have a family, I should imagine it's almost impossible. I think that's why there are fewer women foreign correspondents than men: they are perfectly capable of doing the job, but the demands can be too much if they want a family as well.

I think it depends on your personal circumstances, but generally it's easier to do this type of job when you're in your twenties and don't have commitments.

WORKING ALL OVER THE WORLD: THE INTERNET

To misquote *Star Trek*, cyberspace is now the final frontier. Reporting from overseas to the public back home is one thing, but how about writing for anyone in the world – or at least those with access to a computer?

The technology of the Internet means many of the old certainties about journalism are fraying at the edges. For example, why wait for conventional news bulletins when the first news of major events can be found on the Net? What's more, the Net can even offer a medium for news you would never read anywhere else – whether that is unpalatable truths from oppressive regimes which have no free press or the latest

X Files-inspired conspiracy theory about Kurt Cobain's death or who shot JFK.

This strength can be a weakness as well, though. Many of those posting items on the Net are keen amateurs. The reliability of what is said is not guaranteed – and with terrestrial law such as libel less effective, if not useless, the scope for accusations and inaccuracies, malicious or accidental, is wide. Some might question what makes journalists, who after all are self-appointed, any more legitimate conduits of information; some might doubt their objectivity or neutrality. But it is only as a larger number of genuine journalists' reports appear on the Net that the medium is likely to become recognised as a news provider rather than a general information source.

Such a colonisation of the Net by journalists is under way and has been since the mid-1990s. It started with the likes of the *Daily Telegraph*, followed by other papers, establishing electronic versions of daily titles. Now the *Telegraph* and the rest – not to mention numerous magazines – are trying to develop the service away from producing just on-screen versions of their editions and towards new products. There are essentially two rival schools of thought on development, one suggesting a move towards electronic newspapers, the other stressing evolution into something slightly different from newspapers.

Computer leviathan Microsoft has taken the former route. It has established its Microsoft News UK service as part of its Microsoft Network Internet system. It has signed contracts with the Press Association and other agencies to provide a service updated hourly, so that users can read the latest headlines at the click of a mouse. The added extra compared to print newspapers is the interactivity offered by the Net: readers can e-mail letters and even questions they want the journalists to ask interviewees. Staff will also produce features in response to what readers want. Editor Geoff Sutton says, 'It means we are open to ideas. Most journalists think in terms of doing a story and that's it. We think by using video and computer technology we will be able to bring things to life.'

Meanwhile, the *Electronic Telegraph* is heading in another direction, again relying on the interactivity of the Net but in a different way. Its editor, Derek Bishton, is not interested in providing stories readers can find elsewhere – be that the main newspaper or any other media. He wants to provide information additional to that generally available – a more database-driven approach. For example, he and his staff set up a Euronet web site, run by the *Telegraph*, using the paper's archives to cover the development of the European Union. More specialist topics are likely to follow. Mr Biston told *Press Gazette*: 'Our readers ... [are] happy with the daily publication. What they want is information and background.'

Whichever route is right – and it is possible that both are – electronic journalism is going to become a more and more important medium. That much can be predicted by the calibre of journalist moving into it. For example, the *Guardian*'s New York correspondent, Ian Katz, moved back from America to take up the post of editor of all the paper's electronic products. Alan Rusbridger said, 'The conventional thing has been to appoint an anorak. The *Guardian* felt the only way to make the Internet work as a successful publishing medium is to appoint a top-rank journalist with new media expertise.' The staff at Microsoft are also experienced journalists – from Radio Four, the *Express* and the *Daily Mail* – brought up to speed with the technology.

The increasing momentum of Internet news was shown by a recent survey of local newspaper managers. Two-thirds thought on-line services posed the greatest threat to the regional publishing industry. The main attraction was the commercial possibilities, especially advertising, but the database role also provided opportunities. A third of those surveyed thought the advent and spread of new technology could kill off the regional press.

Even in that unlikely scenario – and even if your sole aim is to work as a journalist in cyberspace – it is important to remember that, whatever form the media of the future takes, the journalistic basics of the past will never go out of fashion: the ability to spot a story, to interview and gather the facts and then to report them. Remember that wherever you first learn those skills – a school magazine, a local paper, a community radio station or one of the biggest media organisations such as the BBC – they will be all that you need to start off in a career which could take you more or less anywhere. And, forgetting computers and other modern technology for a moment, they are the ones you will need to keep with you at all times – the tools of the trade, equally applicable in Manchester or Moscow.

Appendix A
Further Reading

EDUCATIONAL

McNae's Essential Law for Journalists, Tom Welsh and Walter Greenwood (13th edition, Butterworth, 1995). The legal bible for journalists, often seen being consulted in newsrooms the length and breadth of the country. The standard text on media law on almost all training courses

Modern Newspaper Practice, F. W. Hodgson (4th edition, Focal Press, 1996). The essential text which has given thousands of journalists an introduction to everything from journalese to page planning and the freedom of the press. An old friend of many training-course graduates

Pitman 2000 Short Course, Bryan Coombs (Pitman Publishing, 1986). An introduction to one of the main systems of shorthand. Pitman is taught – relying on this book – by some in-house training centres. However, the NCTJ concentrates on the alternative Teeline system for which there is a range of books available.

GENERAL

Press Gazette (Emap Business Communications, 33–39 Bowling Green Lane, London EC1R 0DA). The weekly what's what and who's who of journalism, from local weekly papers to national broadcasters

The Media Guide, eds. Steve Peak and Paul Fisher (Fourth Estate). An indispensable and practical guide to what's what and who's who in the media, updated annually. Gives an overview of the last year's events in each area of the media, as well as hundreds of contract numbers.

REFERENCE

Willings Press Guide (Reed); *Benn's Media* (M-G Information Services). Those looking for the names and addresses of potential employers, whether for work experience, direct-entry jobs or vacancies for college-trained students, should start with either of these comprehensive guides. Most libraries stock them.

Appendix B
Useful Addresses

GENERAL CONTACTS

Broadcast Journalists Training Council, 188 Lichfield Court, Sheen Road, Richmond, Surrey TW9 1BB; tel. 0181-940 0964. The body which oversees the standards of broadcast journalism training courses. It currently recognises fourteen, which offer more than 400 places a year. It also produces a pamphlet, 'A Future in Broadcast Journalism', about getting into the profession.

Chartered Institute of Journalists, 2 Docks Offices, Surrey Quays Road, London SE16 2XU; tel. 0171-252 1187. The smaller of the two journalists' unions, with around 1,500 members. It produces a leaflet, 'What a Journalist Does', to help those who are considering trying to join the profession.

National Council for the Training of Journalists, Latton Bush Centre, Southern Way, Harlow, Essex CM18 7BL; tel. 01279 430009; Internet www.itecharlow. co.uk/nctj/. The print equivalent of the BJTC not only oversees courses but also administers many at more than twenty colleges. About 600 places are on offer each year, roughly 500 pre-entry and 100 direct entry. The NCTJ also produces a guide for aspiring journalists.

National Union of Journalists, 314 Grays Inn Road, London WC1X 8DP; tel. 0171-278 7916; Internet www. gn.apc.org/ media/nuj.html. The main journalists' union offers a range of legal and other advice for more than 30,000 members working on everything from papers to PR. The NUJ offers advice about joining the profession via a booklet entitled 'Careers in Journalism'.

Newspaper Society, Bloomsbury House, 74–77 Great Russell Street, London WC1B 3DA; tel. 0171-636 7014. The general trade association for local and regional newspaper publishers, it takes a leading role in training for print journalists, both in theory and in practice, with close links with the NCTJ. A pamphlet containing advice for would-be journalists is available.

Skillset, 124 Horseferry Road, London SW1P 2TX; tel. 0171-306 8585. Recently established to oversee the training needs of the broadcast, film and video industries, the group plays an important role in the training of broadcast journalists, not least by producing some of the finest, if not the finest, careers-guide material.

University and College Admissions Service, Fulton House, Jessop Avenue, Cheltenham, Gloucestershire GL50 3SH; tel. 01242 222444. With the increasing number of university courses, UCAS will become more important as a source of training information. Its annual handbook gives details of all courses. But remember to check what is on offer and look for NCTJ/BJTC accreditation.

TRAINING

It is impossible to provide an absolutely comprehensive guide to training courses, their requirements, syllabuses and various individual nuances. There are just too many. Likewise, listing every potential employer who might offer traineeships would take a book of its own.

Below are contact addresses and telephone numbers for the main training organisations and the colleges and centres which teach the generally recognised courses, divided into print and broadcast journalism. They are only intended to provide a starting-point for finding out more; the full details of what is on offer at each must be discovered, and assessed, by you.

For details of where to find potential employers, please refer to Appendix A.

PRINT

NCTJ-accredited courses

The following colleges offer NCTJ-accredited courses – or ones awaiting accreditation – in print journalism. The NCTJ produces an updated list every few months.

Contact the NCTJ or the individual colleges to find out the type of course, the duration and specific entry requirements. The minimum qualification for all is five GCSEs at grades A–C, including one in English.

Access courses are among those run at those colleges marked *; postgraduate ones at those marked **.

See also **Journalism degrees**, below.

ENGLAND AND WALES

Brighton College of Technology, Pelham Street, Brighton, East Sussex BN1 4FA; tel. 01273 667788

City of Liverpool Community College *, **, Journalism Department, 70 Hope Street, Liverpool L1 9EB; tel. 0151-707 8528

City University, London **, Northampton Square, London EC1V 0HB; tel. 0171-477 8000

Cornwall College **, Poole, Redruth, Cornwall TR15 3RD; tel. 01209 712911

Darlington College, Cleveland Avenue, Darlington, County Durham DL3 7BB; tel. 01325 503050

De Montfort University, Leicester **, The Gateway, Leicester LE1 9BH; tel. 0116-255 1551

Gloucestershire College of Art and Technology, Brunswick Campus, Brunswick Road, Gloucester GL1 1HU; tel. 01452 426549

Gwent Tertiary College, Pontypool and Usk Campus, Blaendare Road, Pontypool, Gwent NP4 5YE; tel. 01495 333100

Handsworth College *, The Council House, Soho Road, Handsworth, Birmingham B21 9DP; tel. 0121-551 6031

Harlow College **, East Site, The Hides, Harlow, Essex CM20 3RA; tel. 01279 868000

Highbury College *, Portsmouth, Dovercourt Road, Cosham, Portsmouth, Hampshire PO6 2SA; tel. 01705 283287

Lambeth College *, **, Vauxhall Centre, Belmore Street, Wandsworth, London SW8 2JY; tel. 0171-501 5424

London College of Printing, School of Media, Back Hill, Clerkenwell, London EC1R 5EN; tel. 0171-514 6500

Sheffield College *, **, Norton Centre, Dyche Lane, Sheffield; tel. 0114-260 2700

South-East Essex College of Art and Technology, Carnarvon Road, Southend-on-Sea, Essex SS2 6LS; tel. 01702 220400

Sutton Coldfield College, Lichfield Road, Sutton Coldfield, West Midlands B74 2NW; tel. 0121-355 5671

Trinity and All Saints College, Leeds **, Brownberrie Lane, Horsforth, Leeds LS18 5HD; tel. 0113-283 7100

University of Central Lancashire, Preston **, Corporation Street, Preston, Lancashire PR1 2HE; tel. 01772 201201

University of Wales, Cardiff **, Bute Building, King Edward VII Avenue, Cathays, Cardiff CF1 3NB; tel. 01222 874786

SCOTLAND

The first two colleges below are awaiting NCTJ accreditation.

Bell College of Technology, Hamilton, Almada Street, Hamilton, Lanarkshire ML3 0JB; tel. 01698 283100

Napier University, Edinburgh, 219 Colinton Road, Edinburgh EH14 1DJ; tel. 0131-444 2266

Strathclyde University/Glasgow Caledonian University **, Scottish Centre for Journalism Studies, Cowcaddens Road, Glasgow G4 0BA; tel. 0141-331 3000

James Watt College, Greenock, Finnart Street, Greenock PA 16 8HF; tel. 01475 724433

Photo-journalism

Sheffield College, Stradbroke Centre, Spinkhill Drive, Sheffield S13 8FD; tel. 0114-260 2700

In-house training

The following newspaper groups organise in-house training, offering alternative or additional options to the NCTJ.

In the first instance write to the address given, although you may be told to apply to individual editors.

Each of the schemes regularly has places for self-financing students. But anyone considering paying for themselves should expect to pay between £3,000 and £4,000 in fees alone.

Midland News Association, Rock House, Old Hill, Tettenhall, Wolverhampton, West Midlands WV6 8QB; tel. 01902 374 2126. The only in-house centre accredited by the NCTJ is one of the smallest, taking between ten and fourteen trainees each year. The twenty-week course prepares students for jobs on one of the group's twenty-odd weeklies or two dailies, the *Wolverhampton Express and Star* and the *Shropshire Star*.

The Editorial Centre, Hanover House, Marine Court, St Leonards-on-Sea, East Sussex TN38 0DX; tel. 01424 435991. Formerly Westminster Press's centre, now training students from other groups – and a number of self-financing students, who are offered some help with fees – following a management buy-out. Among papers sending students to the two twenty-week courses each year are *The Times* and the *Financial Times*.

Trinity Holdings, Groat Market, Newcastle-upon-Tyne NE1 1 ED; tel. 0191-201 6043. Sharing a building with three big north-east papers, whose executives often assist in teaching the trainees, the scheme has two intakes of eighteen a year. Each course lasts sixteen weeks before the trainees move on to jobs on one of the group's 130 titles, including some of the biggest in the north-east.

United Provincial Newspapers, PO Box 168, Wellington Street, Leeds, West Yorkshire LS1 1RF; tel. 0113-243 2701. In a hybrid of NCTJ-style college-based training and other in-house schemes, UPN offers about ten bursaries at six training courses. Sponsored students have no guarantee of becoming an in-house trainee at one of the group's five daily and thirty-odd weekly titles, but most do – as do another twenty students. All work towards the in-house diploma.

National print traineeships

A handful of national newspapers offer the chance for young graduates to start a career in journalism at the highest levels.

As well as the titles listed below, others have run schemes and may do so again in the future. It is best to monitor the papers, where any details of new traineeships will be advertised, and *Press Gazette*. Most schemes are aimed at graduates, so university careers offices should also have details of any new schemes.

In addition, some newspaper groups, including the Guardian Media Group, offer bursaries for some students on postgraduate courses. The courses concerned will tell you more when you apply.

Of the four schemes below, two – the Press Association's and the *Financial Times*'s – guarantee trainees will be taken on staff at the end of their training.

Daily Express, 245 Blackfriars Road, London SE1 9UX; tel. 0171-928 8000. Between four and six places are available on a two-year postgraduate training scheme. Trainees, often recruited from journalism courses, spend three months at a time in various departments. Contact Jean Carr, deputy managing editor.

Financial Times, 1 Southwark Bridge, London SE1 9HL; tel. 0171-873 3000. A couple of postgraduate trainees are recruited every year. They are sent to the Editorial Centre for training before spending eighteen months to two years moving around the paper. Contact Martin Nielsen, assistant managing editor.

Press Association, 292 Vauxhall Bridge Road, London SW1V 1AA; tel. 0171-963 7000. About five news graduate trainees are taken on each year (as well as one or two for PA Sport). Most are recruited from the University of Central Lancashire, but other candidates are welcome to apply. Contact Harry Aspey, editorial manager.

The Times, 1 Virginia Street, Wapping, London E1 9BD; tel. 0171-782 5000. Two two-year traineeships are offered each year to those fresh from university or postgraduate journalism courses. Learning on the job is supplemented by a spell at college if needed. Contact Elaine Jones in the managing editor's office.

BROADCASTING

BJTC-accredited courses

All the colleges listed below offer one-year postgraduate courses except the University of Central England, which offers an intensive twenty-five-week postgraduate course.

Some may accept candidates without degrees. Check with the BJTC and the colleges themselves.

See also **Journalism degrees**, below.

City University, London, Department of Journalism, Northampton Square, London EC1V 0HB; tel. 0171-477 8230

Falmouth College of Arts, Wood Lane, Falmouth, Cornwall TR11 4RA; tel. 01326 211077; Internet www.falmouth.ac.uk

Highbury College, Portsmouth, School of Media and Journalism, Dovercourt Road, Cosham PO6 2SA; tel. 01705 283287

London College of Printing, Elephant and Castle, London SE1 6SB; tel. 0171-514 6500

Sheffield Hallam University, Northern Media School, The Workstation, Paternoster Row, Sheffield S1 2BX; tel. 0114-253 4610

Surrey Institute of Art and Design, Falkner Road, Farnham, Surrey GU9 7DS; tel. 01252 732286

University of Central England, Birmingham, Perry Barr, Birmingham B42 2SU; tel. 0121-331 6223

University of Central Lancashire, Preston, Corporation Street, Preston, Lancashire PR1 2HE; tel. 01772 893730

University of Leeds, Trinity and All Saints College, Brownberrie Lane, Horsforth, Leeds LS18 5HD; tel. 0113-283 7168

University of Wales, Cardiff, Centre for Journalism Studies, Bute Building, Cathays Park, Cardiff CF1 3NB; tel. 01222 394069

University of Westminster, School of Communication, Harrow Campus, Watford Road, Northwick Park, Harrow, Middlesex HA1 3TP; tel. 0171-911 5000

In-house training
BBC, Recruitment Services, PO Box 10670, London W5 2FF; tel. 0181-849 0849; e-mail recserv@bbc.co.uk; Internet www.bbc.co.uk/jobs/jobsnow.htm. Two schemes, one for regional and one for national network journalists, are run each year. They are advertised early in the year in the *Guardian* and other newspapers but can also be seen on the BBC web site. There are approximately twenty places available.

ITN, 200 Gray's Inn Road, London WC1X 8XZ; tel. 0171-833 3000. The news supplier to ITV, Channel Four and Channel Five, as well as numerous radio stations via IRN, offers training schemes for both television and radio journalists. In total between five and seven trainees are recruited with the guarantee of a job.

Cable companies
Channel One Television, 60 Charlotte Street, London W1P 2AX; tel. 0171-209 1234

L!ve TV, 1 Canada Square, Canary Wharf, London E14 5DJ; tel. 0171-293 3900

JOURNALISM DEGREES

The following universities offer degrees in journalism. These are not to be confused with similar courses in media studies, a subject of which would-be journalists should generally beware.

More information about the courses offered at the institutions listed is to be found in the University and College Admission Service (UCAS) handbook. But full details about each course should be obtained – to check its practical content and accreditation – before any application is made.

NCTJ-accredited courses, or those awaiting accreditation, are marked *; BJTC-accredited courses, or those awaiting it, are marked **.

Barnsley College, Church Street, Barnsley, South Yorkshire S70 2AX; tel. 01226 730191

Bournemouth University *, **, Dorset House, Talbot Campus, Fern Barrow, Poole, Dorset BH12 5BB; tel. 01202 524111

City University, London, Northampton Square, London EC1V 0HB; tel. 0171-477 8000

Darlington College/Teesside University *, Borough Road, Middlesbrough, Cleveland TS1 3BA; tel. 01642 218121

Falmouth College of Arts, Wood Lane, Falmouth, Cornwall TR11 4RA; tel. 01326 211077; Internet www.falmouth.ac.uk

Liverpool John Moores University, Roscoe Court, 4 Rodney Street, Liverpool L1 2TZ; tel. 0151-231 5090

Napier University, Edinburgh *, 219 Colinton Road, Edinburgh EH14 1DJ; tel. 0131-444 2266

Nottingham Trent University **, Burton Street, Nottingham NG1 4BU; tel. 0115-948 6641

Southampton Institute, East Park Terrace, Southampton SO14 0YN; tel. 01703 319000

Surrey Institute of Art and Design **, Falkner Road, Farnham, Surrey GU9 7DS; tel. 01252 732286

University of Cardiff, Wales, PO Box 494, Cardiff CF1 3YL; tel. 01222 874404

University of Central Lancashire, Preston *, **, Centre for Journalism, Preston, Lancashire PR1 2HE; tel. 01772 201201

University of Sheffield *, Firth Court, Western Bank, Sheffield S10 2TN; tel. 0114-276 8555

Two-year HND

Barnsley College, Church Street, Barnsley, South Yorkshire S70 2AX; tel. 01226 730191

Bell College of Technology, Hamilton *, Almada Street, Hamilton, Lanarkshire ML3 0JB; tel. 01698 283100

James Watt College of Further and Higher Education, Finnart Street, Greenock PA16 8HF; tel. 01475 724433

London College of Printing *, School of Media, Back Hill, Clerkenwell, London EC1R 5EN; tel. 0171-514 6500

Middlesex University, White Hart Lane, London N17 8HR; tel. 0181-362 5000

WORKING ABROAD

BBC World Service, Bush House, The Strand, London WC2B 4PH; tel. 0171-240 3456. Many of the World Service's journalists work through from the news side of the corporation. But there are a limited number of openings for those with languages who submit written applications to a particular service.

Reuters, 85 Fleet Street, London EC4P 4AJ; tel. 0171-250 1122. Up to ten graduates are recruited each year for the two-and-a-half-year training course. Applicants, who have to be under twenty-eight and fluent in English and another language, have to write an autobiographical piece as well as test stories and undergo a series of interviews.